My Journey

Reflections on my life in the Bus and Coach Industry

Austin Lloyd Birks

Copyright © 2022 Austin Birks

The right of Austin Birks to be identified as the author has been asserted in accordance with the Copyright, Designs and Patents Act 1988.

All rights reserved. No part of this publication may be reproduced, stored in a retrieval system, or transmitted, in any form or by any means (electronic, mechanical, photocopying, recording or otherwise), without the prior written permission of the publisher.

Bespoke Artwork © 2022 Melissa O'Reilly

The right of Melissa O'Reilly to be identified as the illustrator has been asserted in accordance with the Copyright, Designs and Patents Act 1988.

All rights reserved. The cover artwork and illustrations may not be reproduced, stored in a retrieval system, or transmitted, in any form or by any means (electronic, mechanical, photocopying, recording or otherwise), without the express permission of the artist.

Contributing Editor: Dave Power

Editor in Chief: Viv Ainslie

First Printing, 2022

ISBN: Print: 978-1-8382476-5-2

eBook: 978-1-8382476-4-5

Published by Purple Parrot Publishing

Printed in the United Kingdom

Foreword

Austin's blogs have been lovingly compiled into this superb volume, initially by Austin's partner Yvonne, and then by the team at Purple Parrot Publishing. They are timely, pertinent, acute, and sometimes very funny!

All are worth reading, and indeed re-reading, as he looks and relooks at the UK bus industry.

I hope you have bought this book – if you have, you've made a contribution to the Bus Archive, which looks after the records of road mass transport in the UK. Austin's father effectively founded it and Austin, of course, supports it.

If you haven't; you should – for the reason that it's a great book, and also that you will then be supporting the Bus Archive.

Happy reading!

Peter

Sir Peter Hendy CBE
Chair Network Rail,
Chair London Legacy Development Commission,
Formally Commissioner Transport for London

Dedication

John and Margaret Birks
My parents, who taught us good values to try and live by.

Dr Yvonne Skalban
My Partner, best friend, and soul mate, without whom there would be no book.

Abigail Emma Birks
My raison d'être.

The Journey Begins

Typical...
No Event for Ages, Then Three Come Along at Once!

On Thursday 22nd March 2012 the launch of the inaugural lecture of the Bus and Coach Forum of the Chartered Institute of Logistics and Transport (CILT) was held at the site of the Olympic Village in Stratford, London. This prestigious event was actually three events rolled into one, and I was fortunate to attend.

The first part was a hosted visit around the Olympic Village in Stratford. I was not sure what to expect as myself and 139 others had responded to an invitation from the Bus and Coach Forum of the Chartered Institute of Logistics and Transport.

The tour was by bus and it was a truly excellent experience. However, attendees had to produce their passports to comply with security requirements.

Next was the great bus debate, featuring two of the Bus Industry's biggest names, Peter Hendy, the Commissioner for TfL, the President of the Institute, and Giles Fernley MD, UK Bus Division at First Group and formally Chairman of the Confederation of Passenger Transport. These two heavyweight champions each shared their vision of the urban bus over the following ten years. Once attendees listened to both sides and asked questions, there was a show of hands to determine a winner!

Next was the formal launch of the 2012 UK Bus Awards. This prestigious event has grown from humble beginnings to become the premier event in the Bus and Coach professional calendar. The very experienced team responsible talked through the event's categories and timelines, along with an explanation of how to enter.

Finally, to round off the evening, were refreshments and the chance to network with other friends and colleagues, and best of all, the event was completely free to attend.

In fairness, singly they were three excellent events, but together it was unmissable, and so it proved to be.

However, the visit around the park was quite simply inspirational. I was not sure what to expect before I went on this journey. I had watched the landscape change travelling through to Stratford from my former flat in Poplar and been frankly impressed as the stadiums and venues began to rise, and finally become real. But, in truth, nothing prepared me for the sheer size and scale of the venue, which actually covers four boroughs. From the outside looking in, you get no idea of the enormity and variety of structures. Be they the Stalin-inspired athlete's village, the flowing curves of the aquatic centre, and the sheer outlandishness of the Pringle, but I have to say, the fusion and chemistry of everything to me had a richness of architecture that really works. Populating the site, there are so many trees that it will be the biggest urban forest in the UK.

I came away, after the 50-minute trip, inspired and with a feeling of optimism and pride, this was a British success, on time and within budget. An army of 25,000 worker ants had made this a living, tangible place that not only rose to the occasion in the eyes of the world, but even more importantly, it resurrected the East End, the poor relation to its Western neighbour.

It was apparent that those who were ready would deliver and all the 28,000 employees of TfL, truly tasked to deliver, would do so. Inspired not only by the planning, but also the motivation of being part of something unique and wonderful, as well as the moving video that was played by Peter after the visit. It put the journey experience into context and made me feel proud in the creation of the Olympic Village and the roles of those tasked with making the event come to life. Of course, it would always be about the athletes and those competing, but don't forget all those who made this colossal challenge a success, because that is what it was.

There would never be another chance to actually experience the Olympic Village – a memory that you can share with your grandchildren.

As Max Boyce used to say, 'Yes, I was there.'

Nottingham –
Is it the Best Collection of Operators in the UK?

A discussion once took place amongst a few worthies assembled at an event. It became a lively debate, post-refreshment of the amber nectar, that tried to identify which one location had the best average scale of operation.

Well first, by what criteria does one judge? Is it on average fares, frequency, age of vehicle? As one would suspect, views varied widely. However, there was a consensus that in terms of perception alone (bearing in mind it truly is in the eye of the beholder), Nottingham, pound for pound, had the most colourful cosmopolitan collection of buses.

The joyous rainbows of Trent Barton, the introduction of Scott Dunn's very stylish Yourbus, with their distinctive, John Everill-inspired liveries, along with the Premier and Nottingham City Transport were safe bets, that conspired to portray an impression that other areas didn't seem to have.

Of course, this is never a logical argument as, ultimately, a good area is hard to define. But a couple of hours in the most populated areas normally allows one to create an impression. And I would challenge you, dear reader, to offer your suggestions as to where the most colourful bus services operate. But remember, it is not just one, but all, who serve the fair citizens, so you have to judge the good, the bad and the ugly.

Peter Huntley –
A force for good?

I went to Nottingham Castle as Trent Barton Bus Company had decided to name a bus after a man by the name of Peter Huntley.

He was a big man, he was a clever man and a man of opinion. He was also an excellent example of someone who cared about people. The last time that I saw Peter alive was at a conference in Manchester. I bought him a pint of Guinness and he told me about his latest adventure. He was organising a trip to the South Pole to raise money for charity.

Sadly, Peter never made it as he died tragically after falling while out walking in the Lake District – a freak accident that took a man who was larger than life.

I first met him years ago when he was invited by big Ken Mills, my old MD at Midland Red West, to do some consultancy work. He

was visionary, forceful, bold and funny. I liked him a lot.

He was also one of that rare breed, a consultant who could not only talk about it, he could deliver it as well, as he did with Go Ahead North East. He took some of us around his patch and I was very impressed by what had been achieved. At the end of the trip, he gave us a goodie bag which contained a scale bus that now sits on my desk, in my office.

Like many others, I will not forget Peter Huntley, and quite rightly, he was honoured at the UK Bus Awards ceremony with a category named after him. Very apt and right, he was a bit of an individual in an industry that breeds corporate people.

Peter Huntley was a brand unto himself, and actually, in my view, a really good one.

Dante's Inferno & the Customer Experience!

Way back when I was a Senior Management Trainee with the National Bus Company, I was sent off to Digbeth Coach Station to understand the operations of National Express. A key hub in the organisation and, for me, a regular haunt as a student commuting from Birmingham to Manchester.

One of my abiding memories was the degree of rudeness that I regularly used to encounter from some of the drivers who, for some reason, genuinely displayed what appeared to be a universal hatred for those who boarded their coach.

One in particular, a very big, overweight chap, bedecked in a liberal swathe of both tattoos and gold jewellery, stood out from the others. He almost became a cult figure amongst students who dared to travel with him. He had mastered the art of rudeness to a degree seldom achieved by others.

I could never understand why people put up with him, but he would always seem to be around scowling, muttering and doing what he did best – upsetting his punters; people like me, the average punter.

So, move on one year and I find myself in Digbeth Coach Station in a long black coat and a big black inspector's hat. My job was to patrol the coach station and try to place punters on the coach. This was a frantic operation which really showed the true glory of human panic. Every two hours there would be an exodus of biblical proportions as around 30 coaches, seemingly scattered about at will, would all attempt to flee the coach station. It used to remind me of the scenes that emerge when racing pigeons are released en masse. However, these were no racing pigeons, these were people who were confused, stressed, lost and bewildered, looking amongst the haystack to find their particular needle.

The largest collection of lost souls was the old lady brigade who would stumble about as the minutes and seconds elapsed. It was our job to pounce and then attempt to get them on the right coach. This took nimble feet and good eyesight, and involved gliding the ladies across the congested fume-filled smog of the coach station.

I actually got quite good at it and prided myself on trying to get the punter on board. There would be no time for thanks, just a glint of relief in the eye and then, like a ninja, I was gone.

And then, after the wagons had rolled, would come the silence, and out of the fog would emerge the unfortunates who the system had failed, dazed and confused, only to be told, 'Sorry, love, it will be two hours, best get yourself a coffee and an aspirin, I will come and get you later.'

And I reflect back on the amazing daily ritual of organised panic set against the backdrop of the old Digbeth Coach Station which was a huge blackened cathedral-like structure that had never seen natural sunlight, just the darkness of neon and diesel smoke.

It always reminded me of Dante's inferno, where angels fear to tread, and quick men in black hats pounced on the slow and the confused.

So, today, I celebrate the open beauty of modern Digbeth and I miss nothing of the old!

Stick it in the Family Album...

Well, it took me over half a century, but I finally made it and attended my first ever ALBUM conference and it was great. Well-organised, busy, and it had a really good combination of content and enjoyment.

The deal was simple: the best medium and small-sized bus companies met once a year and investigated a particular theme. This time the theme was (appropriately enough for me with my uTrack hat on!) technology. Or to give it its formal title: Technology, to get onboard the route to success.

It was an impressive gathering and what I particularly liked was the fact that both attendees and suppliers were encouraged to get together, attend the presentations, and interact and mingle. In doing that, a really good and productive atmosphere was generated.

My overall impression was that the Bus and Coach Industry was, at long last, waking up to what the benefits of technology can bring to the table. But, and this was the key, the Industry remained a people business.

The main people who organised it were the good folk of Nottingham City Transport, they who won the best operator award at the 2012 UK Bus Awards. As you would expect, the standard and the quality were of the highest calibre.

So, very well done to Nicola Tidy, the Marketing Manager at NCT, and all the team who made it such a success and Mark Fowles, the highly competent, respected and likeable MD.

And now the gauntlet was firmly thrown down for the good folk at Lothian Transport. I was genuinely looking forward to attending the next ALBUM conference; it truly felt like a family gathering.

Awards...
A Good Thing?

I remember, many moons ago, coming back from school and watching Dick Dastardly and his faithful sidekick, Muttley. They both featured in a classic cartoon called Wacky Races and had a truly bizarre collection of race entrants, including the very glamorous Penelope Pitstop, and the Ant Hill Mob who would resort to *'making with the feet'* if more speed was required, as well as a host of weird and wonderful characters who graced our screens for a number of years in various spin-offs.

The reason I reminisce is simply due to the fact that Muttley's whole raison d'être was about being rewarded with medals at every given opportunity from his partner in crime, the aptly named Dick Dastardly. Such was his single-minded determination to receive such symbols of success that he would inflict serious damage to himself and his hapless master.

So why do I mention this at all?

Well, a few years ago I was going through a spate of nominations for various awards related to the recruitment of Polish bus drivers for First group. Someone I know, who shall remain nameless, said to me in a pub one evening, "Oi! Muttley, what are you drinking?"

Of course, it didn't register immediately, but I couldn't help myself and I said, "Why did you call me Muttley?"

He replied, "Because you are constantly looking to get medals, just like Muttley."

Ouch! I had never considered this before, but it got me thinking. Was I obsessed with craving public success, maybe following the ignominy and stigma of backdoor redundancy? Maybe I was, and then I thought, actually, no. It was because I was both proud and wanted to celebrate our joint success, and have it judged compared to others who were deemed to have created something of value.

I recall attending the first UK Bus Awards, which I think were at Mansion House. A spectacular setting for what has now evolved into a really respected and keenly competed event for recognition of success by our peers in the industry. And hats off to the team who built this worthy event, which is now akin to a 12-month military campaign, but it should be as it is, in the opinion of some, the showcase event. This does not detract from other equally worthy award evenings (Route one in particular), and we cannot forget the excellence of the CILT (Chartered Institute of Logistics and Transport) annual awards for excellence (the clue is in the name!).

However, whatever the motivation, it is clear that as a basic human condition we all want to be appreciated, and one thing for sure is that if you don't enter, you can't win anything. Also, it is not about material gain - there is much more to it than that.

A very good mate of mine received an unsung hero award at a very swanky do in London. He didn't have a clue and the shock was huge, but so was the pride, and when I reminded him how proud his dad would have been, who had worked as a bus inspector in Birmingham all his life, the eyes began to fill.

Because it does matter, it is important, and people value positive recognition. Mind you, he did have the last word, as he took his rather nice certificate and trophy home he turned and said, "This is all very nice, but I can't spend it in Tesco."

...Touché.

The Great Bus Manifesto

I love the House of Commons, it is an amazing place that just drips history, culture and the uniqueness of the British Isles, I have been there about half a dozen times and each time I go I want to stay longer. It's a bit like a drug.

So, anyway, there I was in the splendour of the Churchill dining room, having accepted an invitation from the effervescent and passionate CEO of Greener Journeys, Claire Haigh, to attend the launch of the *'Bus Manifesto: A Manifesto for the Next Parliament'*.

In truth it was full of the great and the good, with a very impressive list of guest speakers aas well as a star-studded audience, including Giles Fearnley, MD UK Bus, David Brown, CEO of the Go Ahead Group, and Martin Griffiths, CEO of Stagecoach, and one of the speakers.

It was a well-organised and worthy event that I felt put the whole bus agenda into a new and, crucially, important perspective. Namely, it truly recognised the vital role that the Great British bus actually plays within the wider fabric of society.

Three simple, but really brilliant, aspirations that I believed were achievable as the tide of public opinion started to reform and it was, in my humble opinion, crucial that we as an industry made it our collective responsibilities to promote, echo and support the cause at every given opportunity.

So, hats off to all those who made this great event a reality.

Preston Bus Station...
The People's Choice

Many moons ago I used to work at Preston Bus station. Back then it was a thriving, busy place with lots of people constantly coming and going. It was a big, imposing building that has constantly split opinion from the day it was built over 50 years ago.

Greener Journeys, I believe, did a brilliant job in putting the role of the bus into its true context with the wider society, and this event went a long way towards recognising that role and celebrating it.

The manifesto promoted three agendas:

- Firstly, to encourage support available to local authorities and bus operators for installing bus lanes and other priority measures.
- Secondly, to propose a bus bonus to encourage people to travel by bus. This would be a new tax incentive to promote modal shift; and
- Thirdly, to see more discounted bus travel schemes for young people, starting off with a concessionary travel scheme for apprentices.

Photo: Mark Mcneill on Unsplash

My recollections were mostly happy although my job was a bit naff. I was a commercial assistant, whatever one of those was, and mostly I had to organise and devise excursions, mainly for pensioners, which was alright; Blackpool, seaside trips, theatre trips, you name it and we went there. It seems odd now in the Internet world that people actually got a simple pleasure from meeting up, spending the day together and doing something different, but they did.

One of my more obscure jobs was trying to find new and exciting events that were a bit different. The one I recall best was the *'Well Blessing Dressing Special',* which took place at Easter, across a range of villages in Derbyshire and involved decorating wells. They were then judged, and an overall winner would be announced.

All good harmless fun and I thought a nice, genteel day out for the nursing home brigade.

So, the day came and went, and as usual on the Monday I met the driver to ask him for his feedback.

"Well," he said, "you excelled yourself there son. All was going nicely until we got to the third village, when suddenly all hell let loose."

What no one knew was that the event was one of the biggest events in the Morris dancing calendar. Traditionally, to mark the well blessing, teams of Morris men would be invited to attend and perform which was great.

"It was like watching a re-enactment of the Wars of the Roses," the driver said. "There were sticks, clogs, blood and carnage all over the place. Most of my elderly ladies legged it as the skirmishes went public. Sixteen arrests were made; it was epic, one of the best days out I ever had."

The only problem was that the ale was flowing and local rivalries got out of control as a pitched battle took place between members based in Yorkshire and Lancashire.

So fast forward 30 years and I read with pleasure that, following extensive public consultation, it seemed that the icon that is Preston Bus Station will remain on the skyline.

It is an altar to a different era and I for one am glad that it will not be confined to history.

What Makes a Good Bus Driver?

Photo: Super-Straho on Unsplash

In all my years involved with this great industry I have often asked myself the question, what is it exactly that makes a good bus driver?

Is it driving skill, appearance, time keeping? Is it how much money they bring in each day? Is it reliability? The list is, I suppose, endless and it all depends on your own personal criteria.

Or is it the X factor, something undefinable? There are certain basics that need to enter the mix automatically, such as regular attendance, honesty, good relations with all around, and a helpful attitude. The list of course could go on and I dare say others might add and subtract accordingly.

But if I had to choose one key element that makes an individual stand out, then I think that I would have to say that it is the ability to make the customer feel valued and special in a positive way.

I have had people who have worked for me in the past who have just been steady good guys. Day in, day out, year after year, they have come in, done a good job and then, after thirty or forty years, they have reached the top of the escalator and finally off they go into the horizon.

A lifetime of service to the communities they support. A key, but often invisible, cog in the daily lives that people live, often unheralded, just taken for granted, a bit like breathing I suppose, but equally valuable.

So, what makes a really special, great bus driver? I think it is someone who makes every single person they deal with better for the experience of having been in contact with them. Very hard to define and yes it is much more than saying hello and goodbye as the passenger gets on and off the bus. In fairness, it is difficult in the tiny amount of time that allows for interaction between driver and customer, but it is possible that people feel better for having had that contact.

The other thing that matters is what I call the feel good factor. Passengers, I think, notice subconsciously how drivers behave. Trust me, if you get a bad or nasty driver the passengers are very aware of the driver's behaviour. It is like everyone tunes in to see what is going to happen next.

Conversely, if you get a great driver, the mood on that vehicle becomes infectious, people feel happier as there is a good vibration. Very hard to define in words, but suffice to say it is that X factor we all seem to crave.

Sadly, the truth is that it is rare, but it does exist and where it does we should respect it and encourage others to pursue it. Wish that I had it... ha!

Passing the Baton

Way back on November 5th 2013, a great event took place at Tubelines' very impressive HQ in the heart of Canary Wharf, in Central London. It featured two of the UK's most successful and admired bus leaders, Roger French OBE, former MD of Brighton and Hove Bus Company, and Sir Brian Souter, the co-founder of Stagecoach and owner of Souter Holdings.

The event was titled *'Passing The Baton'* and was designed to give guidance to the next generation of Young Bus Managers as well as reflections to more mature attendees and, believe me, it did not disappoint.

The presentations given could not have been more different, but that reflected the characters of Sir Brian and Roger, which was also part of the attraction.

Roger French OBE

Roger gave an excellent presentation, which included a fast and fluid collection of images of the big issues and the little details that make a good bus company. It was a passionate, honest and funny testimony from a man who built an excellent bus company because he got the big issues right.

The presentation was a road map that showed, in brutal honesty, where the Bus Industry gets things wrong and, oh my word, had Roger captured that so well. I watched with genuine emotions of humour, horror, pride and shame in equal measure as graphic images flashed on the screen illustrating the often reinforced message from Roger that when we get it wrong, the public quite rightly pass a poor judgement.

The collection of depravities, human ailments and sheer bad taste things splashed across our Nation's buses exposed the simple truth that Roger returned too repeatedly, namely that attention to detail can make all the difference. From the four corners of the land, photos illuminated the very worst cases.

In fairness, companies big and small appeared and no one was immune.

Roger went onto illustrate examples where the industry had got it right and, in fairness, there were some truly excellent bus companies and they quite rightly stood as a beacon and went a long way to restore balance and pride.

This was a presentation delivered with care, humour, passion, frustration and belief. The audience really appreciated what he said and how he said it. As you would expect he set the bar very high, but then again, the next to jump over the bar, was the one and only Sir Brian Souter...

Sir Brian Souter

It was then the turn of Sir Brian, who had a completely different style of approach and delivery after his 41 years in the industry. He had told me that he was not going to use PowerPoint, nor was he going to use any notes and he did not.

No technology required here clearly, but in fairness that is not his style. His take was very simple, he had decided that he was going to try and apply for a job with the Young Bus Managers and he would persuade them why they should hire him. It was the polar opposite from Roger's approach, but that just made the contest more attractive.

He started by giving some background to his career and what his early experiences had been, like when he started as a young conductor and had experienced the worst elements of bad busman's behaviour.

As his experienced old driver had asked him, "What shall we do today laddie? Shall we operate early so the punters miss the bus or shall we operate late and make them wait for the bus."

To which he replied, "Well, could not we just operate on time?"

To which he was told, "That is not how it works."

Well, clearly, he had very different views. His point, which was regularly repeated, was simple; get the basics right and think about serving the needs of the customer. He then relayed his passion about engaging with customers, initially about when he started working for his local bus company. The company policy was not to answer the phone when customers rang.

When he started Stagecoach, this obsession resulted in his answering the phone 24 hours a day, seven days a week, which after seven years, resulted in near exhaustion. As his brother pointed out, sleep deprivation was one of the most effective forms of torture.

The rhetoric flowed as anecdotes and experiences were rolled out, all underpinning his reasons why he should be hired. It was, on occasions, very funny and clearly his astute intelligence, coupled with accountancy acumen and that canny Scottish risk-taking ability, combined to paint a very compelling reason why he should be hired.

What was also manifest was the strong strength of character and purpose that has helped build one of Scotland's most respected and revered entrepreneurs. The range of qualities and experience were quite expansive, but that small edge of individuality that is unique to him also shone.

So the question is, who do you think the audience voted on who to hire, and who to retire?

Hire or Retire?

Following these two brilliant presentations the audience were invited to ask questions. The three young Turks from the Young Bus Managers Network started the batting and they did their network proud as they each asked intelligent and poignant questions that resulted in equally skilled and incisive answers.

The future of technology in the industry, the impact of potential legislation and managing customers' expectations were covered. and we were indebted to John from Go Ahead, Patrick from Brighton and Hove, and Ian from Lothian, for being courageous, challenging and testing with their contributions.

General questions from the floor were then asked for and they came thick and fast: political interference; Liverpool's mayor; loss of subsidised services following austerity measures; they were all in the frame. Interestingly, both speakers blood pressure rose at certain questions and their passions rose as they chose to defend their positions and decisions.

But, and this was key, it was intended to be informative, entertaining, and educational, that's what people came from far and wide to hear and see, and they did. Eventually, after 45 minutes of questions from both the young and old, it was time for a decision to be made. The fun part of the night was for the audience, having heard both presentations and enjoyed the quality of the answers to the questions, now to decide who would be hired and who would be retired.

On arrival everyone had been handed a piece of card on one side was the word 'Hired' and on the other side was the word 'Retired'. The audience had to stand up and hold up either the 'Hired' or 'Retired' card when I said the name. Tension was mounting as I asked them to vote for Sir Brian Souter, they stood and made their choice, and the two counters carefully added up how many hires and how many retires were displayed.

It was then the turn of the audience to decide the fate of Roger French and that they did. I asked for quiet as Daniel and Emma totalled up the scores and they then told me the result.

It was a dead heat. No one saw that one coming, especially me!

I then had to make a decision; do I use my casting vote or do I defer to the result of the crowd? There was no choice to be had, both had been excellent both were winners along with all those who attended.

They both received a mug with the immortal words '*World's Best Boss*' and a pair of slippers. Both options had been covered.

Thank yous were in order for this event: Sir Brian Souter and Roger French OBE; young Bus Managers, John, Patrick and Ian and the sponsors, Martin Griffiths, CEO Stagecoach, and David Brown, CEO Go Ahead Group.

By the same token there were thank yous due from: the Bus and Coach Forum Committee: Lee White, Emma Forde, Daniel Parker-Klein, John Carr and Stuart Smith; CILT, Steve Agg, Allison Glandfield, Tara Betts and Tracey Mathews and TfL, Sir Peter Hendy for the team at Tubelines, led by Beverley Deverish and her great team.

Richard The Third?
No Thank You – I Have Just Had One

I enjoyed visiting Universities with my daughter along with the then current Mrs. Birks. I enjoyed the experience so much that when my daughter had gone to University I considered visiting on my own to adopt a potential student.

I have been to Durham, very nice but a long way to go, Reading, nicer than I thought, Cardiff full of energy and finally Leicester.

The subjects Abi studied were utterly fascinating; Archaeology and Ancient History. One of the joys of the visits to see her were with the presentations and the faculty visits. Truly clever and dedicated people – they all knew their crafts. Naturally it was a massive sales jobs as they seek to attract the best students.

It was therefore a particular bonus that some of the academic staff at Leicester were directly involved with the amazing discovery of the mortal remains of King Richard the Third lying where they had been committed to the earth for all those years. There was an amazing documentary which chronicled the whole adventure. Brilliant!

The incredible find and all that went behind it was a real credit and it was amazing when it was confirmed that following DNA tests that the remains were definitely those of the late King. This made news headlines around the world and put the archaeology team at the

University up front on the World's stage. So I say well done and hats off a truly remarkable achievement.

But as you may know by now I cannot but notice the strange and the humorous in life, and I must confess to having a strange but funny experience while at that University. Basically, one of the key men involved with the find who had been co presenting at the lecture that we attended decided that he needed to answer the call of nature at the same time as myself.

Consequently, whilst I took care of my particular need this chap popped into one of the cubicles in order to partake of the most basic human requirements. Now to this day I have no idea what inspired me but I was reminded quite bizarrely of one of my favourite cockney rhyming slang words, namely when passing solids down south it is sometimes known as a Richard the Third... you can work out the slang yourself.

So, I was presented with a once in a lifetime chance to inquire of this chap as he washed his hands, just what was it like to discover Richard the Third? Did I have the bottle? Well you will never know...

The Passengers' Bottom... Line

One of the strange things that has always occurred to me is just how much thought ever goes into the design of seats when it comes to good old-fashioned public transport. If you think about it, it is the great unconscious aspect of travel that, to my knowledge, never really gets explored. So, why do we think that is the case?

When you pause to consider, your backside is the real customer when you make a journey. You don't kneel down or stand on your head. No, you place your derrière on whatever is offered by the transport company. So, why is there such a huge variance in the design, shape and simple comfort of the average seat?

I always note that when you watch those nice adverts for expensive airlines, they always focus on the luxury of the seat that you are going to buy. American Airlines with Kevin Spacey or glamorous ladies from Etihad Airlines always seem to glide you into the lovely chair that you are going to hire from

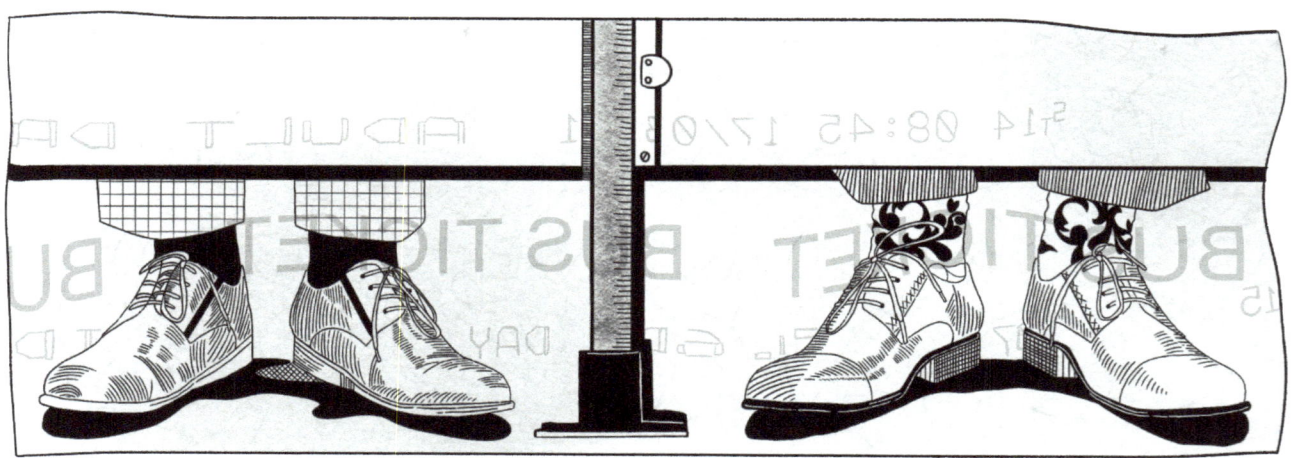

point A to B. So, what then do we do in the UK bus and coach sector to entice people onto our services?

Well, when it comes to sitting down, absolutely Jack in my experience. I remember many years ago in 1987 when I was launching a brand-new fleet of minibuses in Hereford. We had 30 of them all lined up to replace an elderly fleet of knackered Leyland Nationals. I recall with immense pride leading the convoy for a celebratory drive through the historic medieval streets of Hereford, which completely jammed the traffic, causing some unpleasant road rage scenes! Not quite the impact that I had intended!

However, although happy with the seat provided to the driver, I had not considered the impact of the design on the rear end of the punter. Much to my horror, when we entered service, we were far from receiving the expected plaudits about how great the new fleet was, instead, I received complaints about the size of the seats of the minibuses compared to the Nationals, which almost offered park bench-sized receptacles for the average bottom, in comparison to the pert seats provided by Mercedes. However, when it came to the minibus, it was all about maximizing the seating, so, sadly, the punter took second place to the economist who wanted volume at the expense of basic passenger comfort; the one thing that should always be a priority.

I remember one of my drivers complaining bitterly about a bad day when elderly ladies with bigger padding had been bemoaning the demise of the National as he transported them on the bingo special. He said to me, with a degree of passion remembered to this day, "For God's sake, gaffer, can't I take one of the old buses out? I don't think I can take another day of moaning about how much their backsides hurt."

Sadly, there was little that could be done to alleviate his woes. Of course, over time, the complaints evaporated as the smaller seat became the norm and Hereford Hoppers went about the daily business of taking punters from A to B!

"For God's sake, gaffer, can't I take one of the old buses out? I don't think I can take another day of moaning about how much their backsides hurt."

Ferry Across the Mersey

My few, enjoyable, visits to Liverpool have left positive memories, namely visiting a pub called The Baltic Fleet with my mate Johnnie Mackin, a lifelong Liverpool fan. We went to watch Brighton play Liverpool and, as a Brighton fan, I had to be physically restrained when Brighton scored as I was standing in the Kop (circa 1982).

Afterwards we trotted off to this strange pub in what today is the very nice Albert Dock district, but back in the day the place was run down and derelict. The first thing that I noticed was that the pub had a parrot that welcomed you in a broad scouse accent. In truth it might have been the several beers that had previously been consumed in several other hostelries beforehand.

However, Merseyside has undergone a series of changes. Post-deregulation, the region now operates a very coordinated and efficient bus network with Arriva and Mersey Travel offering what seems to be a harmonious and sensible bus network.

Such features as a coordinated timetable, enhanced evening and Sunday bus services, inter availability of ticketing, strongly branded with the Q Brand, there is a real sense of structure and prolonged partnership.

In fairness, another excellent example of joined-up thinking. If only everywhere enjoyed the same benefits.

Kithead Trust
A Worthy Cause

I was at an excellent conference recently, hosted by my dear old friend James Freeman. He was a top bloke and not surprisingly it was a really good event. The attendees were members of the Young Bus Managers Club, the bright young things who would shape the future of the Bus and Coach Industry.

I went down there with my good mate Chris Ruanne from the CILT as I was given a ten-minute slot to talk about the six-month free membership offer that members of the club had been generously offered by Steve Agg, the CEO of CILT. The reason why I managed

to blag this spot was care of my very dear friend David Beaman who was presenting about his fascinating life and times in the UK Bus Industry as well as to highlight the work done by the Kithead Trust.

This is an institution that was founded by my dad, John Austin Birks (big clue in the name there!), 25 years ago. It was established to house the records of bus companies that, in many cases, had long and memorable histories. However, so many companies back in the day (post de-regulation in 1986) were getting sold off left, right and centre, meaning that these vital records were ending up in skips.

Fast forward 25 years and it now houses a massive collection of truly historic records that capture our transport heritage over, in some cases, 200 years. The issue now is that it is reaching a crossroads, as it is manned by volunteers and is at a point where it needs to gather momentum, so it can be accessed more by academics, students and the like.

So, David talked with humour and passion about the Trust, and his last photo featured my dear old dad. I therefore thought it very fitting that I kept the image on the screen as I talked about why it was important that these young guys especially need to join, and at the end of it Chris had the names of 16 recruits, not bad out of 36, so it was a job well done, and all under the watchful gaze of my dad.

He would have liked that.

Blackpool
Fun, By The Seaside

I had the pleasure of revisiting that bastion of the Great British seaside resort that was so popular back in the good old days before the world changed out of all proportion. I once blogged about my managerial experiences in the fair resort and what a life-changing experience that was!

However, it had been many years and as I drove up with some friends I was not really sure what to expect, and as it was my birthday I was naturally enough in high spirits. So, we turned up and booked into a very friendly hotel slap bang in the middle of the place. You could almost touch the famous Blackpool Tower.

After checking in we had a swift half and decided to venture out into the heart of the place. Regrettably, the weather had taken a decidedly worse turn, with the wind howling in from the sea and the sky had gone grey. The shops were boarded up and the garbage

was dancing its merry way along the roads.

Unable to find a hostelry that was deemed suitable, we found ourselves stumbling into a German beer cellar, ironic as I was with my German friend, Yvonne. We both found it highly amusing especially as it was empty.

I bought a couple of rather tasty beers, and asked the barman where everyone was. "Oh well, the young farmers are in town for the weekend, there are thousands of them, so make the most of the peace and quiet mate."

Sage words, wisely delivered. Within minutes, the first posse had arrived being led in, sheep dog style, by a young lady very scantily dressed as a fraulein. The men who accompanied her were mixed in age, however, they all had one thing in common. They were all completely blotto.

Within minutes, loads more groups had joined them, all suitably intoxicated, and before I knew it, one group started to dance and then wrestle with each other, managing to throw beer down the back of my shirt. Oh, and by the way this was at half seven in the evening.

Well, that was it, it set the tone for the weekend. The sheer volume of drunk people with absolutely no inhibitions staggered and beggared belief. The young farmers clearly don't seem to get out much as they seemed to behave like Vikings who were marauding the village.

To be fair, there were many maidens waiting to be pillaged – I think the modern parlance is hen parties. I gave up counting the number of times I was flashed at, if you know what I mean.

In truth, I really don't know what it is that gets people to behave like that. Of course, beer is the key, but there is also a sense that anything goes, because it is Blackpool, which it is. One chap thought that it would be good sport to moon at the diners in McDonald's while they tucked into their nuggets.

To be fair it was not just a quick moon it was a prolonged affair that would at least cover both a starter and main course, and this is the thing - no one really took any notice. I mean would you do that in, say, the bank?

I think the whole thing was summed up for me when at 10:30 on Sunday morning I strolled off to get the car where I had to pass by a group of girls from the young farmers. They all had bright pink t-shirts on and were drinking San Miguel. They were having piggy back races followed by pavement wrestling competitions. Now, it may be a young farmer thing, but it actually resembled a scene from military re-enactments. Bit like the Sealed Knot recreating the battle of Worcester during the English Civil War, except it was 15 girls on the pavement in Blackpool, some of whom could not get back up.

I have nothing but the utmost respect for the good folk of Blackpool. They endure these antics week in week out, they are truly unshakable and equally un-shockable, unlike me. Clearly, I am getting old, maybe I need to get out more...

A Humbling Process
Meeting Your Staff From Years Gone By

Hereford Crematorium is a place that I used to attend on a rather regular basis back in the days when I was a depot manager, but some 22 years on since I said goodbye to the lads and lasses who used to drive, day in, day out, often in fiercely competitive circumstances, I was back once again to pay my last respects to my dear old mate, Howard.

As I drove into the car park the hearse was in position and as I entered the place I saw the tall figure of Andy Todd who had been kind enough to track me down and let me know of his passing.

As I walked in and looked around I saw a lot of old faces, then I spotted one of the lads, Nigel. He had not changed at all and immediately came up and said hello. After the short, but fitting service was over we all gathered outside to pay our respects, and then, one-by-one, faces that I remembered once as either young or indeed middle-aged men and woman came into view and it was a genuine joy to shake them by the hand and to look them in the eye.

They told me that they meet once a month for a few beers and a bite to eat, and they very kindly invited me along; there were some amazing memories to share and catching up to be done.

What was most touching was that some of them said that the years we shared together were the best and, on reflection, I have to agree with them. I took my role very seriously. I considered them as a family and we all genuinely cared for and looked after each other.

That was the ethos of the Midland Red family and, even after all those years, it was as strong as it ever was. I always said that good depots were tribal, they were like families. Yes, you had your off days, but most days were good and lots were excellent.

Basil Fawlty Runs a Bus Depot

I am not normally a man who loses his temper, and indeed, those close to me would agree that such occurrences are rather few and far between. In truth, I am not actually very good at it and often tend to apologise as soon as it's over, irrespective of who is responsible for instigating such behaviour in the first place.

It is very rare, and with my regular exercise regime, I believe that it helps to keep one calm and able to carry on in the face of life's adversities. However, on occasions, when employed as a manager or a leader, one has to be strong and show leadership, especially in such a male-dominated industry like the good old bus and coach.

Indeed, I know of one well-known operator who used to keep a baseball bat behind his desk, in order to sort out 'people problems' as he used to describe them. It always struck me as a tad over the top and used to conjure up images of Bam Bam from The Flintstones. In fact, I had images of this chap randomly wandering around the depot taking pot shots at drivers, fitters, or anyone really who happened to be in the way.

What was it that inspired me to 'lose it'? Well, we need to go back to 1988 when I was working as the Depot Manager for Hereford, and life was comparatively easy. I had a good team who knew what they were doing, and most days were good. However, things were about to change. One of the services that we operated under contract to Herefordshire and Worcestershire County Council was to the Sixth Form College, and in fairness, it was usually not a problem, but one day the driver comes back with a complete seat panel cut to pieces with a Stanley knife, or some other implement.

This was utterly unacceptable, so the next day, I went straight over to the principal to express my unhappiness.

He asked, "Do we have any idea who was responsible?"

The answer was no.

"Well, there's only one thing for it. We will get them all together and you can investigate properly."

Oops, I didn't see that one coming, but fair play, if he was up for it then so was I.

So, the next afternoon at 15:30, I turned up with my inspector – a huge bearded former firefighter who genuinely did not like people very much. Looking back, I have no idea why I appointed him, but I did.

We wandered into the main hall to be confronted by 60 students. The principal introduced me and explained that someone slashed the seat, which, by the way, I was holding as if it was an exhibit at an auction. This was my cue – we'd agreed that we would play a bad cop, bad cop type of tag team.

So, off I go on my rant.

"I would like you to imagine that I have just walked into your home, gone into your lounge and then started stabbing your favourite chair. Yes, imagine that, because that is exactly how we feel about whoever has done this. And it is one of you people standing here."

At this point, I am now behaving like Basil

Fawlty on one of those comedy TV shows. As I brandished my mortally wounded seat around like a demented banshee, eventually, having exhausted myself, I took stock of the situation. A sea of sullen-looking young faces stared back at me and just behind me, I can hear the sound of giggling as my inspector is barely able to conceal his mirth at my out of character outburst.

Ignoring him and making a mental note to slash his overtime, I stared back and then out came the classic line:

"No one is going home until I find out who committed this wanton act of vandalism. It is my bus and whoever killed this seat is going to pay for it. So, if it was you, and you know who you are, then now is the one chance that you are going to get to confess. If you do that now I will not pursue charges with the Police. Show some courage and be responsible for your actions."

Well, you could hear a pin drop. Absolute silence.

Then, from out of the blue, a voice pipes up, "It was me, I slashed the seat," as a gangly tall youth stepped forward to take the rap.

For a second, I was reminded of the classic Kirk Douglas and Tony Curtis movie, Spartacus, and was fully expecting others to stand shoulder to shoulder and proudly chant, 'No, I slashed the seat' but no such luck.

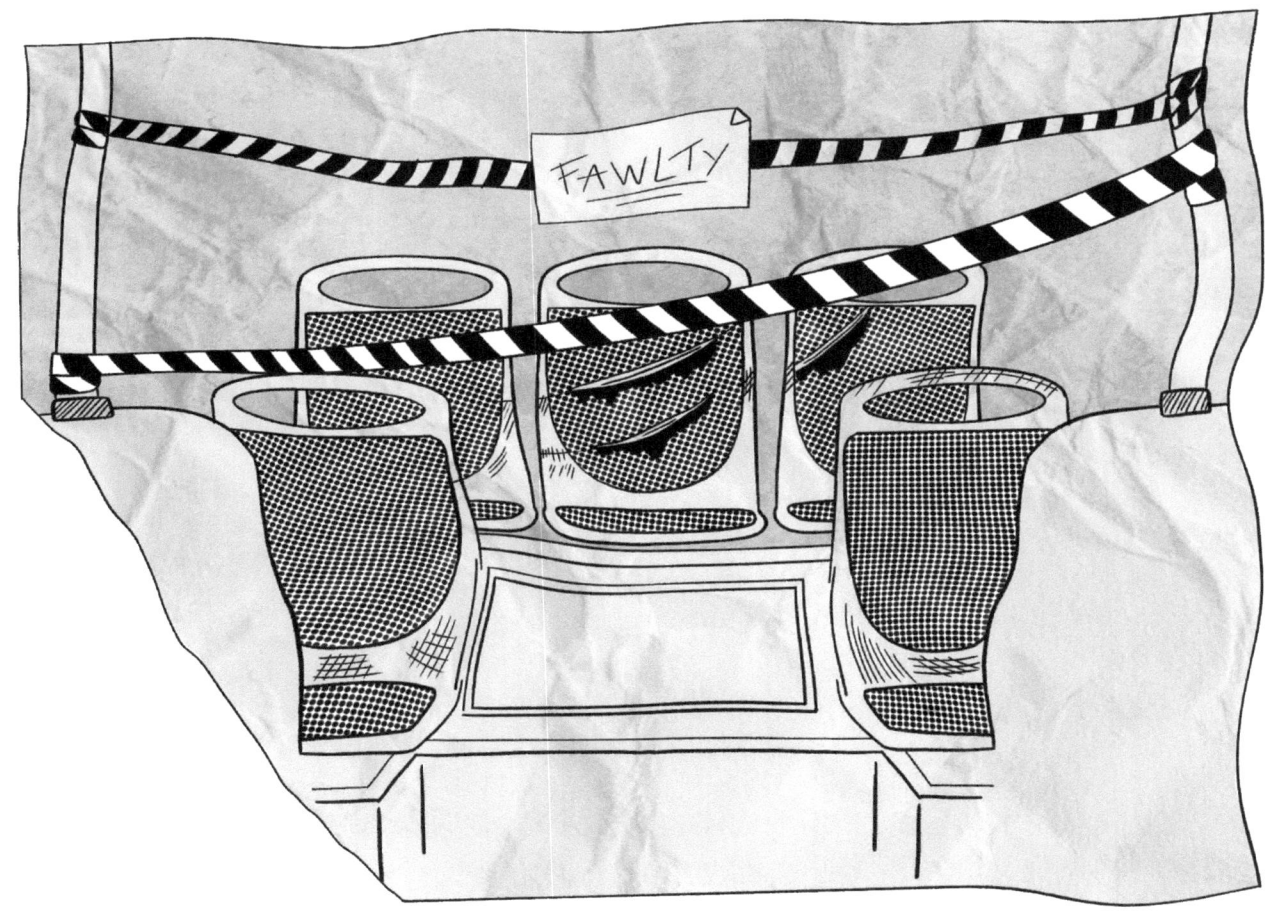

We had our prisoner, now the next question was what to do with him.

"OK," I said, "I appreciate that you owned up, your punishment is that you will be banned from using the bus for two weeks and you will have to pay for the damage."

Looking back, ideally, I should have donned a black hat, not dissimilar to those worn by Victorian judges as they announced the death penalty.

And so, with honour restored, the sullen youths sloped off to the delayed bus while the principal, offender, inspector and I went back to his office – in my case, mostly for a well-deserved gloat.

Easily pleased, me.

The Impudence of Youth

I was scanning the many TV channels that this modern age has allowed us play with when I stumbled across a documentary about Blackpool in all its past glory, and it got me musing on my three-month deployment when I was at the good old Ribble Valley Motor Services. Ribble was once a mighty empire and one of the larger companies that once formed the National Bus Company.

I'd been given, what they call in footballing parlance, a 'free transfer' or last chance, to be more accurate after I had decided to commit professional hara-kiri at one of the infamous three-monthly reviews that all NBC graduates were subjected to at the grand and palatial offices in Victoria, Central London.

The deal was quite simple, a two-year training programme where, once every three months, the trainee would submit a report and then the nine-man panel of senior general managers and directors would grill the hapless soul who was sat before them. I was 18 months through mine and progressing quite well at West Yorkshire Road Car Company in Harrogate when the fateful day arrived.

I spent my three months with the engineering department doing nothing useful with the engineers, semi-skilled fitters and apprentices. Poking bits of buses, handing over washers and plastic things to men in dirty overalls who loved nothing more than to fix buses. I spent a week in the stores understanding the importance of good stock control and robust auditing. As usual I filled yet another note-book recording my uselessness, which of course would never be opened once it was confined to a dusty cupboard.

I think that I was feeling a bit disillusioned and was not ready for the interview. Even worse I was the last to be interviewed and it was after lunch. This was never good news because, for the panel of seniors, it was usually a four-pint affair depending on who was there. There was one man on the panel who was known as the Yorkshire Terrier, two clues in the name. He was the hard cop, and loved to intimidate, ridicule and stress candidates, and today it was my turn.

So, in I popped, sat down in front of the largest board room desk in the world and prepared myself. Pleasantries were exchanged as the chairman handed me over to the Terrier on a large platter.

"I read your report, it was rubbish…" was his opening gambit

Silence.

"And, why was it rubbish?" I enquired.

That was mistake number one.

"I counted 13 spelling mistakes," he replied, as his face visibly reddened as I was answering back.

"Did you actually read what I wrote then or were you simply looking for mistakes?" I was on a roll now. "What was the content like? Was that rubbish?"

Silence descended.

Those asleep were nudged awake as the air of confrontation thickened.

"Don't be clever with me lad, you just remember where you are," he bellowed. "You're not here to question me. *I* will ask the questions."

More silence.

"How many spare windscreen wipers are kept in Bradford depot?" he then shouted.

Mistake number two – do not, under any circumstances, giggle.

"Well," I said, "if I told you there were 30 would you know if that was the correct answer, because neither of us have the faintest idea? And come to think of it, why would either of us want to know? Is this what a Captain of Industry needs to know?"

Giggling was now breaking out with the nice members who were enjoying seeing me standing up to the Terrier. Well, that was it, he went ballistic. I only recall a great deal of noise, in a four-pint Yorkshire accent. I definitely recognised the word *impudent*, and several other words of what is best described as Anglo-Saxon for the purposes of editorial decency.

Eventually, drained he stopped.

A moment's silence, then the nice Chairman said, "Mr Birks you will now leave the room while we consider if you have a future on this scheme."

You could have heard a pin drop as I attempted to walk away with dignity having just realised that I had possibly gone a bridge too far.

The nice man in charge of the trainees quickly ushered me away into the side room where the other five remaining trainees were waiting. They had heard the commotion. In fairness, if you had been in Birmingham you could probably have heard it. Not a word was said as we walked through into another office. My residing memory was watching this chap walk back into where the other lads were standing looking through the door staring at me. And then, very slowly and deliberately, the door was shut and the faces faded away.

Well, I thought, that must be what it is like when the curtain closes at the crematorium and you are on the way down... which actually made me laugh. An hour later, I was called back in to see the Chairman and the nice mentor man.

"Well, Austin, we have not witnessed a scene like that in the history of the graduate training scheme. You certainly divided opinion quite dramatically. On the one hand, some viewed you as impudent and you should go immediately. However, others took the view that, as a senior manager, you need to stand up for yourself, and they thought that you did just that. In confidence, your reports have been consistent. You are clearly a people person and the question asked was can you be tough enough to handle yourself? And we felt that you did, however, we want to get a second opinion, so we are going to send you to a different company and give you some management challenges and see how you get on. So, as from Monday, you will report to Frenchwood in Preston to meet the General Manager, Mr. Ian Chapman.

And that, my friends, is what I did and he turned out to be one of the nicest men I had the good fortune to meet. He, of course, was in Lancashire. My days in God's Own County were sadly behind me. But everything happens for a reason.

Rewards For Awards

So, picture the scene, it is Tuesday night at the Organza nightclub in downtown Warsaw in the heart of Poland. Some 350 people have crammed into the club to attend the biggest, best and, indeed, first ever National Recruitment Awards. To see just who is the best of the best across this fiercely competitive market that is so crucial to the development of the ever-expanding Polish economy.

I have a good friend who I nominated for an Unsung Hero Award, and I watched his tears flow when completely surprised he was invited onto the stage at the London Hilton Hotel in front of 750 people to be recognised for his lifetime of dedication.

As he got up to go I said to him, "Just think what your dad would have thought."

That was why he was so moved, it meant everything to him and so it should. The point being that no amount of money, or indeed

success, can really compare against being recognised by your peers, your competitors or indeed your industry. The genuine look of happiness of those that were chosen by an expert panel of industry veterans was indeed a joy to behold. The thing is that subconsciously we all, even if we chose not to admit, like to be recognised as being the best that you can be.

After a lot of seriously hard work by the team at Verita, led by the super-efficient Ola and her team, the whole process of drawing up short lists, selecting judges and organising the venue, finding sponsors, sourcing prizes, and the hundred and one other essential tasks that need to be carried out to make the event a success, were dutifully completed.

The result was a well-organised, enjoyable event. It was well attended and became a must have fixture in the Professional Recruitment Industry.

It was really important that best practice and innovation are recognised and shared with not just the industry, but with the whole of Poland.

My personal congratulations went to the following winners:

- Antal and Adecco - the winners of the Large Agency Award
- Devonshire - the winners of the Medium Agency Award
- Bergman HR - the winners of the Small Agency Award

Congratulations were also given to all the companies that made it onto the shortlist, a real achievement in itself, and I hope that rather than be disappointed they pushed that bit harder so that the following year it would be their name engraved on the rather nice trophies.

The funny thing was that all of this was formed on the back of a night out in Wroclaw with myself, Andy Samu and about four other guys who met for the first time, had a few drinks and ended up late at night in the Papparazzi, talking about planning an annual event. Indeed, my hazy memories of the night included a certain Tomasz Szpikowski, the owner of Bergman HR who won one of the awards, amongst others, myself included, who ended up dancing on the bar in the Pap.

Album Conference 2015

Busmark... Out of the Blocks to a Flying Start!

So, for the third year I was fortunate enough to spend four days and three nights at the ALBUM Conference, hosted by Network Warrington, care of MD Damian Graham and his team, headed up by Gina.

As ever, it was really good, the hotel was excellent; modern, set in truly beautiful grounds and with all the amenities you would need. My role, along with Mr Fixit, Chris Ruane from CILT, was to both man the stand, so that we could attract members, as well as (on the last day of the event) formally launch Busmark, along with Mrs Beverley Bell, the senior Traffic Commissioner and the new President of CILT.

The were two thing about ALBUM which made it so good in my opinion.

First, the calibre of the presentations of which there were many. They covered a diverse range of subjects, and in fact I noticed that Sir Brian Souter, in his truly excellent thought-provoking speech, highlighted the ALBUM Conference as one of the Industry's biggest and most important events. I have to say that I completely agreed.

The second thing that I really liked was the social element. This was equally important and enhanced my belief that the bus and coach community was, indeed, a big extended family. This was the big family reunion where old friendships were enhanced and new ones were forged. Not only with fellow operators, but with the small army of suppliers who supported the event, and it really was great fun.

There was a choice of activities: archery; shooting; segway; golf; a pub quiz and Bullseye style game show – truly something for everyone. At the gala dinner, out popped the famous 70s comedian, Stan Boardman (famed, for his Fokker German plane gag of World War II).

He was on good form and made lots of golf jokes the best being, *'The only balls I hit properly today when I was on the golf course was when I stood on a rake.'*

The launch saw members of the Busmark steering committee give brief, but passionate, endorsements for membership. They included Adrian DeCourcey, Martjin Gilbert, Alex Perry, Richard Hall, John Carr, all incidentally Fellows of CILT, and Chris Darby from Marsh Insurers who had taken up the role of Gold sponsors and very kindly donated £10k to the cause along with Silver sponsors, Mix Telematics, Lloyd Morgan Group, and Omnibus Systems who contributed £3k each.

The result was that £19k was raised by Busmark which would subside membership of Busmark to only £250 per organisation as compared to £895 for membership to Logmark – the widely respected and long standing Logistics and Freight benchmark club.

The Busmark project was two years in the making, from an original meeting held in Corby where some 20 operators from the UK and Ireland assembled to map out how the club would work. As a result, a smaller committee was drafted in to create the content which resulted in seven specific sections which captured the infrastructure of the Bus and Coach Industry. They included Operations, Engineering, Operational Risk and Safety, Environment, Employees and HR, Technology, and Customer Service.

The final survey contained 90 questions completed once a year and would be expertly analysed by the team at Corby, headed up by Daryl Chesney and ably supported by Katie Workman and Chris Ruane, who would send the results to each company as to how they compare to their peers by means of a traffic light-style system (red, amber and green).

The first survey was completed in 2014 with an impressive 35 companies, large and small, across the length and breadth of the UK taking part, which was indicative of the significant interest that Busmark has generated. Indeed, it already included 13 members in its ranks since launch, with many others looking to get involved.

So, the collection of some 150 individuals from a range of 50 excellent companies were the fifth largest group in the UK Bus Industry with between them over 5,000 vehicles. They had a simple ethos; membership was by invitation only, and they were looked after by a small, but highly able, committee serviced by long-standing secretary, Thomas Knowles, supported by President, and all time good bloke, Ben Colson, and John Owen OBE, the Godfather of all things good in the UK Bus Industry.

Membership excluded the big five groups as they liked to cherish their independence and added a professional voice to the other bodies who represent the Industry (CPT, CILT etc).

Utrack on the Winners Shortlist Again...
and Score a Hatrick

So, it came to pass that one Friday we received an email from the charming Tara from CILT to say that uTrack software solutions had been short-listed in the Information Management category of the highly respected Chartered Institute of Logistics and Transport Excellence Awards.

Now, I was very fortunate to be invited to the previous year's awards which were held at the really rather grand Lancaster Gate Hotel opposite Hyde Park in the very heart of London.

The event itself was, as you would expect, a highly regarded prestigious affair with the great and the good from across the whole transport spectrum. Black tie and ball gowns were the order of the day, with some of the most senior people in the transport world, including the likes of former president Sir Peter Hendy and Mrs Beverley Bell amongst others. So, to have uTrack up there being deemed worthy of being short-listed along with two other entrants was really rewarding.

The thing was that this time we were being judged against the best that was out there in the rail, aviation, maritime and haulage industries. Indeed, you name it and we had been decreed by an independent panel of expert judges as being worthy of recognition.

I had given up trying to second guess the award results. Every time I'd tried to work out where we would end up I got it wrong, so clearly I was not very good at it. I would simply enjoy the event for what it was and if we won then that would be excellent, but if we didn't then I would be just proud that the team had been recognised across the transport profession as being worthy of consideration.

When the time came, the event was held at the Lancaster Gate Hotel. Again, the gentlemen were all attired in dinner jackets and the ladies were resplendent in gowns. The event was well-organised with the team at CILT in Corby doing an excellent job.

I didn't think that we were going to win. My instinct said quite simply 'no, uTrack will not win', given the scale and reputation of our fellow finalists.

As I had learnt, my instincts were rubbish as yet again at exactly 22:21 a nice man opened an envelope and, to my sheer surprise, out came the immortal words,

"And the winner is... uTrack Software Solutions."

Well, like a young gazelle in springtime I was off. I was vaguely aware of events around me, but my main concern was to make it to the stage without calamity.

Next, I am shaking hands with the excellent CILT President, Jim Spittle, being given a lovely heavy-duty glass trophy and having my photo taken. In truth it was all a blur, and over in seconds, but it meant a lot because this was now the third time running that awards we had entered and won.

And yes, it was a good feeling; even better for having been faced with that sting of disappointment of coming second or being highly commended in different awards in the past.

It is only human nature, but what for me was so remarkable was that this was a real team effort at uTrack, with each person bringing value on board that ultimately was judged as good by one's peers. I never took these things too seriously, but for myself and others in the team this was the flip side of a long and, on occasions, arduous journey. It had been peppered by set-backs, but none of us involved lost belief that we were doing something that was adding value to the industry that we found ourselves engaged in.

So, in one year, 2013, uTrack won the UK Bus Award for Innovation at the Hilton Park Lane, the Innovation Award at the UK Coach Awards, came second in the Making the Coach Accessible category, won a Better Choice award and then uTrack won the CILT Information Management Award with Coach Tracker and National Express. Over 4 million people had used uTrack technology on a variety of devices and we thank Tom Stables, Kevin Gale, and the rest of the team at National Express Coach for their help and support as we jointly shared the success of our partnership.

Whatever Happened to Good Manners?

I was once in London attending a meeting with some very nice chaps from one of the big five bus groups. As a result, I felt compelled to wear a suit, which does not happen very often these days in my non-corporate world. Two things about why it is not a good idea to wear a suit in London: one was the steaming humidity of one of those ghastly sticky days; the second was the peak time travel overloading on the Tube.

Now, don't get me wrong, I am a big fan

of the Tube and tremendously enjoyed an excellent BBC documentary which showed the truly day-to-day heroics of all those who make the magic work. It is rare that I am ever disappointed (don't get me started on Wizz Air, by the way, nine hours late in Luton Airport!).

In fairness, the travel experience is usually pretty darn good, but there is one thing that I have noticed and I suspect it is a generational thing. And that is that I seem to find myself increasingly offering my seat up to ladies or elderly people, who look like they would appreciate a seat.

Now, there are certain protocols that you have to manage. Do you give up your seat to a lady? Because when I was brought up, it was automatic. No. These days, you have to exercise some discretion as some ladies do not seem to want to be offered a seat.

One lady, when I offered, said, "I am not pregnant, I am just fat."

I did not know what to say, it never even occurred to me that she was pregnant... queue muffled silence and slow sit down with eyes fixed firmly ahead to ignore the eyes now staring deep into my embarrassed soul.

Anyway, there I was on the Circle line, which was fairly empty until it got to Baker Street, where a huge mass of humanity was waiting for the doors to open before they all surged on - the cosmopolitan folk who make London what it is, a melting pot of humanity.

I was quite comfortable perched on my seat when, in front of me, six hot, sweaty elderly people got on looking flustered and squashed. So, I immediately stood up and offered my seat to the nearest lady who thanked me, called me a nice young man (shades of Dick Emery for those old enough to remember) and sat down.

This was when the trouble started as one of the gents turned his attention to a group of four young people.

He said in a very loud voice, "Did you see that? He gave his seat up to the lady, why didn't one of you do that?"

Oops, the great British convention was massively breached; under no circumstances ever say out loud what everybody else thinks and would like to say, but cannot because they are British.

What happened next?

Nothing!

They just completely ignored him and carried on, utterly oblivious.

So, what are we to make of this? Do we damn all young people? No, of course not. There are many good people out there who are up and down like yo-yos to help others out. But conversely, there are others in society who would not put you out if you were on fire. The vast majority are probably somewhere in the middle, and I for one will not stop giving my seat up.

Graduates...
Good or Not?

I note with interest that the major transport groups have had greater numbers than ever before applying for places onto their graduate entry schemes. Both Stagecoach and First had trumpeted the fact that not only were more and more young graduates applying, but it meant that the quality and calibre were, hopefully, better than ever. This was always good news for the Industry, but did it potentially distract from those who had worked hard to come through the ranks and were demonstrating real ability and flair?

Well, the answer should have been no, of course not. Good businesses should always be looking out for talent and grooming accordingly with a steady eye on succession planning. A quality business should also, depending on its size and scale, have been more than able to facilitate the training and required skills to take people with talent and ambition to the next level. And, of course, had they failed to look after them, then the good would go.

I remember my dad giving me some advice as I was about to go for my eight-man panel interview for the National Bus Company Senior Management Training Scheme in London, donning my new suit and hat (don't even go there with the whole hat thing).

Anyway, the advice was *'look them in the eye, give a good firm handshake and call them Sir. If they ask about your degree, focus on English Literature not drama; these are bus men you're meeting, not members of the Royal Shakespeare Company.'*

Thanks, Dad.

Indeed, my effort to look all of them in the eye as the questions came in thick and fast from the eight-man desk must have made me look as if I had some deranged manic stare, rather than the honest, *'I will stand my ground like the man I am'* face that I think he was wanting.

But, hey ho, the last question was from a gentleman called Fred Dark, a legend of the National Bus Company whose trick question was, "Well, young Birks, if you don't get in, what will you do?"

"Well, sir," I replied, lining him up with

my steely stare, "I have put in an application to get a commission to join the Royal Air Force."

"Ah, jolly good, going to be a fighter pilot like your brother, is that the plan? Although I can't help noticing that you seem to have a lazy eye. Either that or you're a bit bug-eyed, can't have you lining up the sites with one eye akimbo, Lord, no."

And on that note, the interview was over, and I was in. After all, they were all friends of my dad who was the ninth man on the panel and who had stepped out for my interview to give me some advice.

Nepotism. Keep it in the family I say.

Female Bus Drivers
Where Are They & Why Are There Not More?

One of the great ironies I've always felt with bus drivers in the UK is exactly why there are so few women driving buses?

What is it that actually stops women from thinking, *'I could do that'*? Is it the male-dominated 'macho' image that still, for some reason, pervades today when many other sectors appear to have shed this image (the Police and armed forces being good examples)?

Or is it the shift work, a possible perception that it might be risky? It's hard to find a definitive answer, however, why is this not the case for the women who work on the tube, or indeed the railways. What is it about the bus or coach?

It is time some serious thought went into this issue, especially at a time when some bus companies are still recruiting from outside the UK, which is fine, but what about employing mums, misses or, indeed, Mrs?

Well, hats off to People 1st, a training company who have recently successfully placed ladies into bus driving jobs. Many years ago, while working for a bus company in the Midlands, I recall talking to the prison service to see if we might be able to engage women coming out of short-term custodial sentences for mostly non-payment of debt - simply preposterous, but we do like to lock people up.

Of course, it got laughed out of court when I tried to sell the idea to the hairy-chested medallion wearers who used to run the depots.

They were very sympathetic... not, and

these were the same people who, when we moved bus services into a well-located Tesco bus station, were virtually kicked out due to the overzealous sexual harassment that took place when they were allowed access to the subsidised canteen. It's unreal, you could not make it up.

So, let's go right back to the image of the bus, with the rather sleek new Borismasters stirring up the public's imagination. Maybe there should be some serious thinking about employing those who we actually carry the most. Why not set up B&Q-style academies for female bus drivers, or perhaps focus on the increasing lost generation of 16 to 24-year-olds who can't get jobs. If we select, motivate and train them, why not?

None of us have anything to lose!

The Real Benefits of Transaid...
Life Changing Causes

I was fortunate enough to be invited to an inspirational event hosted by Eversheds law firm; one of the largest and most successful law firms in the UK. It was an early kick off, with access from 09:00, so to make life easier I stayed overnight, just down the road, at a place in Paddington.

So, bright-eyed and bushy-tailed, with my best bib and tucker on, I presented myself at the rather palatial offices, got signed in and went up to the seventh floor to enjoy the spectacular views that the glass walls allowed, as the building is virtually next door to Saint Paul's. It certainly was a wonderful venue for what was about to unfurl across the morning and the early afternoon.

As HRH the Princess Royal was the guest of honour, it was no surprise to see four police officers with their sniffer dogs checking out all of the offices in close proximity. The security that surrounds such royal visits is really quite amazing. However, it is worth recalling that HRH was once almost the victim of an IRA kidnap attempt in the 1970s where she showed remarkable courage and famously told her prospective kidnappers to Foxtrot Oscar... a real chip off her dad's block.

So, the scene was set, I helped myself to a coffee and then mingled, as you do, with other attendees. I met one chap who was quite remarkable. Neil was a bus driver/trainer who went off to Tanzania for a six-month secondment to teach people to drive buses. This was inspired by the immensely high mortality rate due to poor training, so this gentle giant of a mild-mannered Scotsman, who worked for Stagecoach, decided that he would do something about it.

Six years on he had not come back and later he was shortlisted as an unsung hero at the UK Bus Awards.

I met some really interesting and decent people at the event, and they all had one thing in common; to foster and support Transaid in however they could.

There were several presentations about the great work being done by Transaid across Africa. But the one project that really resonated with me was the work done to save mothers in remote villages, where too many mums and babies died as they were unable to access medical help that we just take for granted. What Transaid did was build bike ambulances; mums were taken across sometimes rough terrain to medical centres to get vital treatment. A simple concept that worked and saved many lives. One lady was transported over 20 miles on the back of a bike strapped to a door, she received the vital help she needed and both her and her baby survived.

Truly remarkable stuff and I came away inspired to do more to help.

Londonderry
Inspiring and Humbling

I was extremely lucky to be invited to a conference hosted in Northern Ireland. In truth I had not been to Ulster before as I don't count driving through Belfast from a ferry crossing to attend the Rose of Tralee festival in 1977 when we were all either drunk or asleep, as a visit.

So, I was really looking forward to the experience, which was organised by the super Tony DePledge, a non-executive director of Translink, and key personnel from the Bus and Rail services teams who were responsible for the state-owned entity that served the good folk of Northern Ireland.

The trip was clearly split into two very different parts. One was some excellent presentations about the bus and transport scene in Belfast and across the country. The other was an understanding of the troubled history that had existed across the centuries and, indeed, in the recent bout of 'the troubles' as they came to be known. All of us on the trip were surprisingly English and we all, I believe, came away from the visit with a new and deep-found respect for those involved in the tragic events that I clearly recall marking my formative years.

You need to see and experience for yourself the proximity and deeply felt, entrenched emotions that existed in the past. Twenty years after the ceasefire, and the devolution of power-sharing, the people of Northern Ireland were eventually able to bring normality and

Photo by K. Mitch Hodge on Unsplash

hope to the modern generation and those who lived through the pain of the past.

There were many moving and highly eloquent examples, but the one that really struck me was the enigmatic tour guide who walked us, in glorious autumnal sunshine, around the walled City of Derry / Londonderry. As he called us to attention at the parade ground of the former British Army barracks, he explained that he was going to give us a tour of Derry/Londonderry and the bloody history, both old and new, from the Battle of the Boyne in 1613 to the events of Bloody Sunday in the '70s up to the present day.

As he calmly and professionally spoke he then said something that stopped me in my tracks.

"On that infamous day of Bloody Sunday, 14 people were shot dead by the British Army and the 13th to get killed was my Dad!"

It was a shocking and sobering statement that made the past very real.

The tour was absolutely brilliant and I would highly recommend it to anyone, the guide was engaging, well-informed, sometimes very funny and often very sad. But what really came home to me was this man's sense of genuine and passionate optimism and complete lack of bitterness, and true belief in the reality of a safe and prosperous future for Ireland.

Truly humbling and inspiring.
What a good man.

Temper, Temper!

One of my more bizarre memories of my lifelong journey in the world of bus and coach was triggered when I watched a rather strange scene when I was travelling on the Underground. I have to say, that in all my life I have seen very few examples of the dark side of the human condition. However, in a nutshell, an argument broke out between a group of youths, they did not seem to know each other and I have no idea what instigated it all.

The upshot, however, was that a really nasty exchange took place that did not quite break out in violence, but it got very close to it. As all the spectators were captured in a moving carriage, no one could get away or even choose to ignore it. The whole thing was short, sharp and brutal with anger, and loud shouting and swearing. As several young men squared up to each other and the atmosphere took on a menacing and dark turn, it reminded me of a very odd situation that I once witnessed in the old head office that I worked in once upon a life.

The background was simple enough. An ordinary day; me and three others sharing a large office all doing our little bit to keep the machine moving. One of my fellow workers was a highly intelligent and able man, although by his own admission he did have a short fuse, and like volcanoes, occasionally the man would explode.

One Thursday afternoon I was in the secretary's office talking to the PA to the MD, Big Ken Mills. There was a man from BT busy doing something under a desk and generally minding his own business. He was the first casualty, as without warning a very loud and angry shout suddenly emanated from the hallway. BT man, like all of us, immediately shot up. Sadly, as he was under a desk, he whacked his head extremely hard and was the first man down.

I went straight out to be confronted by my angry friend holding the long metal coat hanger stand, minus coats, being used as a lance to break the glass in a door. I could see that the red mist was down and decided upon a timely retreat, closely followed by the lady secretaries who showed a remarkable turn of pace as they collectively legged it in the opposite direction. Women and children first was the order of the day as the sound of breaking glass and guttural bellowing broke the usual peaceful silence.

Indeed, one lady showed an almost swan like quality as she appeared to glide across the floor, seemingly a foot above the ground, in a rare moment of elevation not witnessed since the magic of David Copperfield at his height... literally.

As panic broke out, I peeped around the door to see the figure-head whirling towards the main door, leaving a trail of debris behind him as timetable cases were knocked down and plant pots despatched with a carefully aimed whack from the lethal coat stand. I gingerly followed him towards the door where he proceeded to vent his anger on some rather nice bushes that nestled either side of the grand doors that graced the entrance.

I then went back to my office to watch the man, finally spent and exhausted, stop and take stock of his handy work. It was as if a small, one-man typhoon had been unleashed. From previous experience I knew that it was best to just let him be and come back to his senses. After five minutes I sounded the all clear to the ladies who had taken cover in the cellar, which was lockable from the inside.

They resumed normal service and myself and the boys from marketing set about repairing the damage, broken glass, shattered doors and broken plant pots littered the floor. Truly a scene of devastation from a clearly troubled soul, I let him be as he sat on the grass, and then made him a cup of tea.

Now composed he asked me what he should do. I suggested that he just went home as clearly he was in a bad place. So without a word he got up and drove home. The next day he was invited to meet Big Ken. I don't know what was said or what happened, but it was never referred to again.

So, my friends, my unpleasant experience somehow took me back to that strange day back in Worcestershire on the day when the dark side was allowed out of the bottle.

We all have an element of this as it is the nature of the human condition, the trick is to try to keep the lid on.

UK Coach Awards
A Great Celebration

I was fortunate enough to attend the seventh UK Coach Awards hosted, as ever, by the excellent team who bring us the equally excellent UK Bus Awards (Chris, Ian, Trevor, Jamie, Pat, Margaret, you know who you are!). I have to say it was an wonderful evening held in the Mercure Piccadilly Hotel with its panoramic backdrop of Piccadilly Gardens in the very heart of Manchester.

After a dreadful drive from Birmingham Airport to Manchester, which took over three and a half hours, I got to the hotel just in time to check in, get my whistle and flute on, and straight down to the bar for a well deserved snorter. As ever I bumped into lots of familiar

Photo by Chris Curry on Unsplash

faces, and within moments it was time to find table 19 and see where my guest and friend Adrian DeCourcey had got to.

As it happened, Adrian was standing next to me, so we took our seats, made our introductions to new friends and enjoyed a really excellent three-course meal. However, there is, as they famously say, no such thing as a free lunch and I was there for a reason. It was soon time for the awards and I was to present the award for the Young Coach Industry Professional.

Now, the protocol at these big dos is quite simple:

1. make sure that you do not drink too much so you do not make a falling over monkey of yourself;
2. do not say anything offensive;
3. make sure that you can read the name when you open the envelope; and
4. do not drop said trophy when you present to happy faced award winner.

There, easy as that, I always have a clear idea in my head what I am going to say, the only problem is that for some odd reason what comes out of my gob is not what my brain had prepared.

I remember a man I liked and admired very much, one Tony DePledge OBE, who I bumped into after presenting an award at the UK Bus Awards his words still make me laugh to this day.

"Ah yes Mr Birks I thoroughly enjoyed your presentation, you displayed all the integrity of a game show host."

Well I cannot argue with that! Anyway my dear chums I digress as usual. So there I was on the stage next to the very tall winner from National Express Coach, a nice man called Charlie Hacher who very clearly has a great career ahead of him. For some reason, when I read his name out I had a huge desire to say and the winner is Charlie *he bit my finger* Hacher. What was slightly different was that while me, Charlie, and my old friend Bill Hiron, Chairman of CPT who was giving out the gongs and is an all round top bloke were standing there having our photo taken, suddenly out of nowhere the lovely Carol Kirkwood, the national treasure who announced the weather on BBC breakfast, dashed over to get herself on the photo, a sort of selfie without her own camera as it were. Apparently they call it a photobomb.

The other rather odd thing is that there was a raffle for Transaid, one of the two excellent charities that CILT fostered, the other being Aspire which is equally brilliant! That year uTrack were sponsoring the annual bike ride known as The Celtic Challenge; it started in Wales and then went over to Ireland on the ferry, through the beautiful Irish hills and finished up at the gates of the world famous Trinity College in Dublin.

Anyway, the deal was that you put at least a tenner in an envelope and then Bill picked the lucky envelope. There were four prizes: two iPads; an Auto Glym pack, whatever one

of those is; and The Footplate Experience the magic of a working steam locomotive. Well, as I sat there watching the iPads get nabbed suddenly Bill said "And the winner of the Footplate Experience is from table 19..."

Hello, I think I am on table 19 and then, I could not believe it, he said my name.

Oh Lord this is awkward, I thought. Not only is Transaid part of CILT, but uTrack are sponsoring the event. So up I jumped like a young stag in springtime and galloped to the stage to request that as I had a vested interest I would like to hand it back and let someone else enjoy the experience. Which they duly did.

Honour restored I thought. Mind you, as the good Doctor said, all very noble Mr Birks but would you have been so quick off your feet had it been an iPad Mini... well hell no, is the simple answer - my lead-based deep sea diving boots would have been firmly strapped on for those beauties let me tell you.

> Comment of the evening came from Barry White of AJ Gallagher and Liberty, who sponsored the UK Coach Operator of the Year Award, who, when giving his very entertaining closing address, described Carol Kirkwood's ample cleavage as resembling, and I quote, "Tightly packed isobars..."
>
> Benny Hill meets On The Buses.

Greece
A Tragedy and a Triumph

I'd never been to Greece before, so when I landed on a very warm and sunny Sunday morning, to enjoy a rare beast, a holiday in the sun (homage of course here to the Sex Pistols immortal ditty from the late '70s), I was both curious and excited to be visiting a nation that had enthralled me since I could learn to read. The epic gods, fables, battles and heroes, let alone the culture, education and poetry. And, of course, the politics (itself a Greek word) of this country that had played such a pivotal role in shaping the history, culture and civilisation of mankind as we know it today, would certainly make this a most engaging experience, or so I hoped.

Such was my boyhood fascination that I used to enjoy wearing a bronze coal holder as it was known (minus the coal of course) on my head, as it vaguely resembled the classic Greek helmets worn by the warrior heroes of old. This of course allowed me to pretend being the ancient heroes of Greece re-enacting my own versions of epic battles between the gods and heroic mortals. When you are six of course this is perfectly normal behaviour, but as I discovered when attempted in my late 40s in a Cotswold antique shop after a few lunchtime pints of Speckled Hen, was frowned upon by those fortunate enough to witness my re-creation of the battle of Thebes.

Five days on and I had travelled the length and breadth of this extraordinary nation, I witnessed extreme contrasts. On the positive it is crammed full of history, signs on the

main highways regularly pointed out temples and theatres that have not changed since civilisation began. On the other hand, I was saddened at the real economic deprivation that litters the landscape, closed down farms, ramshackle buildings, scores of desolate factories and plants are testimony to the reality of economic austerity. It is a sad paradox that the birthplace of civilisation, philosophy, and culture was reduced to an economic scarecrow, even the thriving sea port of Thessaloniki, where we were based in the rather grand Porto Palace hotel, was surrounded by empty and decrepit warehouses and offices. Like everything else in Greece, they were covered in graffiti; an art form of protest that was everywhere.

What I also found surprising was that we were almost the only tourists around. We travelled to one of the most beautiful places in the World, the unique monasteries built against all human odds by the devoted monks and nuns on the spectacular mountains of Meteora.

We drove for four hours past the snow capped Mount Olympus, to visit these amazing buildings and then, along with only four Australians and two Americans, we took an incredible three-hour tour in a minibus the highlight of which was the setting of the sun against the backdrop of the monasteries.

The tour guide told us how these devoted men and women painstakingly built, from the 11th century on, these once 26 churches of God on this impossible terrain.

The reality was that in 2018, only six monasteries remained – history, empires and wars had reduced them one by one.

And today virtually no monks and nuns actually live there anymore. The solitude and isolation that they craved so they could reflect and serve God away from the World, had ironically created a tourist trap that attracted people like me. I had become the spectator on a world of privacy that drove them away from what they had created.

In many ways this kind of summed up

the sadness of Greece. The nation, like the monks, had built a beauty and a heritage that ultimately they could not sustain and was now a shadow of its former self, where ironically people like me have become both the problem and the solution. The future of Greece is dependant on tourism and here I do hold some hope, it is one of those nations that people should visit as its footprint is so vast across all parts of society that many of us owe it a debt of thanks.

What Would the UK Bus Industry do Without Foreign Workers?

One of the interesting things for me about the UK Bus Industry is the unmistakable fact that it has always been at the cutting edge of recruitment from foreign shores. In the '60s, West Indians, who were of course members of the Commonwealth, were invited to the UK to work as bus drivers. In the '70s a lot of people from India and Pakistan also came to the UK to find work and many ended up working as bus drivers.

So it was not surprising that in the noughties, when the EU opened up its borders to allow virtually unrestricted access to members of the newly enlarged EU, that many came to work as bus drivers. Indeed, I admit with pride that I played a pivotal part in establishing a process that selected, trained and placed over 3,000 people into First-group for which I received an award from the European Union.

We engaged fairly and properly with genuine people who wanted nothing more or less than to have a job and do it well, and 99.9 % did just that. These people made a vital contribution and, indeed, all these years on they have stayed in the UK and made new lives. Their children are as British as I am, although many are multi-lingual which I wish I was.

I remember when I was at school, one of my friends was a chap called John Lukaszwich, he was Polish, his parents had escaped from Poland when the Second World War kicked off, yes that is how old I am. The landscape of the UK has changed dramatically since I was born when Britain was a very different world. Today's Britain is hugely cosmopolitan, embracing cultural diversity that can only enrich this nation.

The options open to people living here are enormous. Our history has been built on accepting people who have come to this nation, from the Romans to the Vikings, to the French, its character has been shaped by a constant fusion of different cultures, all adding to the greater good. I was in Ireland and Poland recently and Ireland is very similar to the UK, a really vibrant, energetic place and Warsaw is also similar, being a capital city and sharing that sense of energy.

So I proudly lay my cards on the table and admit that, in my opinion, our industry has been enriched by those workers from different nations.

I remember a partially sighted lady who said to me, *'I really do not care who drives the bus so long as someone drives the bus'.*

Good point well made methinks.

Worcester
Wet But Undefeated

A spell of truly appalling weather brings out both the very best and, on occasions, the worst of the great British public. However, the one place that has been featured the most in the national media has been my old stomping ground, the fair city of Worcester.

A rather beautiful city that boasts a beautiful cathedral, some wonderful medieval buildings and was the site of a major battle during the English Civil War where Prince Charles just escaped from Oliver Cromwell's army. The other key feature is that the city of Worcester sits slap bang in the middle of the River Severn.

Consequently, in days of extreme weather as we just experienced, by the time the River Severn gets to Worcester after it has collected all the new water from its source in the Welsh valleys and mountains, it has inevitably resulted in widespread and severe flooding. There is nothing new in this, but this time it hit an unprecedented high with the river rising 17 feet from its normal depth.

The TV coverage, however, concentrated on the implementation of the British Army; and the local shuttle bus service that was able to ferry passengers from one side of the city to the other, so keeping the shops open and trade flowing. Indeed, this later resulted in the new sport of flood tourism where people flocked from beyond Worcester to marvel at the impressive sight of nature flexing its muscles and showing just how defenceless the human being is in the bigger picture.

It is always good to see the humble bus featured on national television doing what it does best, keeping communities together and helping to promote a normal life in extraordinary circumstances. Well done Worcester and its local bus companies.

Leadership
The Real Test

One of the benefits of working for different companies is that you get a chance to reflect on how different people manage others. I always find it intriguing to watch how those in charge choose to manage their people. As a result, I have always attempted to utilise a style of management which is empathetic – not to be confused with pathetic.

I recall doing one of those HR personality tests which naturally I had already dismissed as utter nonsense, and low and behold it was actually completely accurate and told me where my strengths and weaknesses sat and what I needed to concentrate on to be a better manager. Of course, it went in one ear and came straight out the other.

Ironically, I have observed some of the very best and the very worst. The worst was truly abysmal, a genuinely nasty man who, although clearly not very bright, was cunningly evil. He worked on the principle of imbuing fear amongst all those who were unfortunate enough to work for him. In fairness he had got it down to a fine art. You know the sort of guy, your heart sinks on a Sunday night when you know that you had to see him on a Monday. In fact, he reminded me a bit of the crocodile from Captain Hook, but rather than make a noise like a clock, he had these metal staples attached to his shoes, so you could hear him coming from miles away.

He also had a completely loose fuse and would lose his temper at anything. Looking back, I now believe that he had an advanced form of Tourette syndrome. In truth I had never heard such creative use of swearing. Sometimes this resulted in a strange merging of certain words that was almost poetic. He once rang me and started screaming down the phone at me, I was struggling to understand exactly what the reason for the abuse actually was. What I did understand was that he was personally going to get into his car and deliver not just a round of Fxxxs but, to my undisclosed joy, I was to be given a wheelbarrow full of Fxxxs.

I was desperately trying hard not to start laughing as I tried to visualise what this might look like when eventually the phone was slammed down, and silence descended. True to form, in he drove at speed, jumped out of his car, shoes clattering crocodile like as he strode his way manfully towards my already hidden secretary, who'd done a runner.

Beauty is in the Eye of the Beholder

The door burst open to reveal an apoplectic, red-faced tinder box about to explode. "What the Fxxx do you think you're doing?" was his opening gambit, but before I could offer any reply he was busy bellowing the next insult. It was a bit like being bawled out by a Regimental Sergeant Major I would imagine. Eventually he ran out of puff and turned on his heels and was off, I still to this day have no idea what I had done to inspire such hatred, but after a while I got used to it. Remember dear chum I had been married for many years so was quite used to being shouted at! (Only joking.)

What I could never work out was how this man kept his job, but he did and for years he was still there bawling and shouting, and scaring people, small animals and anything else that he came into contact with. Still, it taught me one thing, how not -to manage, how not to treat people and how not to behave. Good leaders manage and inspire, they do not bully and undermine.

Is it possible to view a bus and find it attractive, or indeed ugly? Well, frankly, yes is the simple answer, and how do you create an attractive bus design? Is it an aesthetic question or a simple 'I like that colour, it will do?'

When I was at Diamond Bus, we decided that we wanted to create a unique identity that combined memories of the Midland Red Bus Company in Worcestershire with a modern, new, fresh, 21st-century flair. Similarly, we desired something bright, innovative and head-turning for the Black Diamond brand to operate in and around the Black Country.

We went to Ray Stenning, who created an iconic brand both for his buses and himself - a true individualist who lived by his principles. I first met Ray when he attended a meeting at Worcestershire County Council. His style and flamboyance, especially set against the leafy conservative drab predictability of the elderly lady Tory councillors, was a joy to watch. Quite frankly, they never stood a chance.

I was a big fan from that moment on and watched and admired the significant and influential impact that Ray and his team have had around the country ever since. I also believe that his whole ethos towards design and perception have done a lot to subconsciously elevate the public's image of the bus and its status in society.

Imagine being sat behind an old, truly knackered, Leyland National. Bits hanging

Handbags at Dawn

Some of my happiest years were when I was the Depot Manager at good old Hereford Depot, where I spent seven very good years of my life. I was young, carefree and enjoyed that liberating sense of self-confidence that you exude in your formative years and truly believe, as Arthur Daley famously said, that *'the world was indeed my lobster!'*

What I enjoyed the most about it all was the day-to-day interaction between all of us involved, like the cleaner, Porky Pig as he was known; his dad was reputed to be General De Gaulle who had been billeted close to Hereford and had apparently enjoyed Ugandan relations with a lady cleaner, none other than Porky's mum. And he had a big hook nose to boot.

The thing was, you never really knew, day in, day out, just what was going to happen. It was a daily play with different characters appearing on the stage each with their own story to tell. Often it was the simple basics: covering duties for those who went sick, sorting out the wages, ensuring that the money was calculated and banked, arranging the rotas, managing the swaps; all the daily functions that make a job a good experience, not a bad one.

This was varied in the extreme, as it required dealing with the human condition in all its bizarre glory. A lot of it was straightforward, agreeing to not too simple requests – I always worked on the basis of if I can I will, but if I cannot then no. However, at other times it could get very complicated.

off dirty, and fumes gushing out from a ropy exhaust, etc., then compare it to being sat behind a bright, clean, Go Ahead Oxford gleaming, modern bus, in a fresh red livery with a clever, witty image and caption extolling the virtues of clean air (again, one of Ray's finest).

It is not hard to understand how one will think about the bus set against such dramatic contrasts, the Industry by nature, in my experience, is conservative. I believe that we need the Ray Stennings, and others with his flair and vision, to elevate our stature, and what I say is more power to your elbow, Mr Stenning.

One particular incident involved one of the elite, as they were known. The elite were the small band of brothers who operated the National Express coach service from Hereford to London and back. Often this required overnight accommodation in London, so the driver and his lady hostess companion would pop off, do the business as it were, and return the next day.

All was quiet one cold November afternoon, when I was summoned by a distressed Melvyn, the chirpy cleaner who had legged it into the office and said, "Quick gaffer, I need you in the canteen, all hell has let loose."

I immediately dashed to the canteen where I was confronted by two ladies engaged in hand-to-hand combat on the floor. Hair grabbing, slapping, and obscenities flew in equal measure, as Melvyn and I did our best to end the scrap and try to restore some order.

Eventually we managed to end the melee and I escorted one of the ladies, who I did not know, into my office and away from the scene. Melvyn took charge of a lady called Suzy, who was one of our three lady hostesses. I sat the lady down, who was understandably very distressed, introduced myself and offered to make a cup of tea.

Having composed herself, the lady explained that she was a wife of one of the elite, who, having found some ladies knickers in her husband's overnight case that morning, had been so infuriated that she had come straight to the depot to confront the lady concerned.

"And who," I said, "is the lady concerned?"

To which she replied, "Well, it is her, is it not? It is that Angie."

Oops!

"I see," I said, "I understand that, but the only

small snag is that the lady that you accused and attacked is not Angie, but someone who, to my knowledge, is happily married."

A slow, rather pained look descended across her already troubled brow as she realised the implications of her haste.

I left her with her brew and a chocolate finger biscuit and went back to the canteen to check on the welfare of said lady. She had composed herself and told me that she was sat having a coffee and a fag, having popped in to see if she could change one of her shifts, when this woman burst in, shouted at her and began slapping her whilst waving what appeared to be ladies undergarments.

She had no idea who she was or indeed what it was all about and had attempted to defend herself. I then explained what had happened and asked her if she wished to pursue formal charges with the Police. No, she said, she did not want the hassle.

I then went back to the wife who asked if it might be possible for her to apologise, which I hoped that she would do. To cut a long story short, apologies were given and received, the good lady wife went home and waited for her husband to come back where she duly set about him with a broom handle causing concussion.

Local folklore, had it that she eventually caught up with the lady hostess concerned who very soon afterwards left the job and moved to Port Talbot where I gave her a reference for a job as a barmaid.

The joys of depot life, you never know what is around the corner.

Just like EastEnders.

Mindless Vandalism

I once watched footage of a bus that a random passer-by had just nonchalantly hopped on board and released the handbrake. A very casual action that resulted in the unmanned bus rolling backwards and crashing into cars and boats that happened to be in its path. Such acts leave me almost lost for words.

I mean, what on Earth is the point? Is it funny? Is it bravado? I cannot for the life of me work out the logic behind it. However, one thing that is certain is just how dangerous and utterly irresponsible the action was. What if a child or anyone for that matter had been in the way? They would not have stood a cat in hell's chance. Sadly, for me, I have seen close up exactly what happens when a bus collides with a human being, and surprise, surprise, the bus *never* comes off second best.

You never forget your first fatality and I have witnessed more than my fair share, most notably in Crown Gate Bus Station in Worcester, when I got a phone call at our old head office at Heron Lodge from the duty controller to say that a driver had been run over as one of the inspectors had reversed a bus off one of the stands. As the accident had literally just happened, I jumped into the car and went straight to the bus station. I got there at the same time as the BBC local news team arrived at the scene.

What I saw was horrific and I was almost physically sick. The bus had gone over the driver and the impact was at the top of the body across the head and shoulder region.

Even worse was to come when I had a microphone shoved into my face and was asked what had happened. The dreadful thing was that they were actually filming the site of the collision with the body still in sight. I mumbled my way through the questions until the Police intervened and moved the BBC away from the area.

Looking back, I was in a state of shock. However, the professional head took over and detailed reports were taken. The poor inspector who had been at the wheel was arrested and taken to the Police station. He was not charged, but as a result of the accident, significant health and safety procedures were launched.

I returned to HQ to brief the MD, Ken Mills, who remained professional and calm, although, like all of us, saddened and shocked at the loss of a friend and colleague. The next thing to do was make contact with the next of kin. The driver's wife worked in a local hotel, and, eventually, I was able to contact her having been assured by the Police that they would inform her of the tragedy and their family liason team would be there to help her.

I rang the lady up, introduced myself and explained that I was ringing to see if there was anything that the company could do. She had not got a clue what I was talking about as the Police had not been in touch, so I had no choice but to tell her what had happened. It was truly dreadful moment.

So, to the funeral. It was as horrible as it gets. In Worcester, the depot closed down and all the staff from the depot and head office formed a line from the road to the entrance of the church. We stood in silent tribute to one of our own. Most poignant was the inspector who was involved, he was distraught as one might expect. The deceased families were magnanimous in their understanding. In fact, a year on, a memorial was erected at the site to remember a good man who had lost his life tragically.

Anyone unfortunate enough to witness such a tragic, sudden and gruesome death, would almost certainly have been extremely happy to share the experience with the three idiots who thought that it would no doubt be a good laugh and let the handbrake off.

The next time, such antics could have resulted in a completely unnecessary accident, meaning another family would have to cope with losing someone when it was all so avoidable.

The Great Uncertainty

I remember once talking to a really nice posh lady at a public event in central Birmingham, organised by Bus Users UK and my old mate, Mr Phil *'mine's a bacon sandwich'* Tonks. She said to me that she would happily catch buses if she knew that they would actually turn up. She was not concerned when they turned up, but that she would not be standing there staring into space stressing about if the damn thing arrived at all.

And then she said, and this was the killer, "Because, in truth, I know that my car will always be there ready for me whenever I need it, but I can't say the same about the bus."

Food for thought, and to be fair, she was right. The eternal dilemma for bus user's has always been *'how can I really know where the bus is and how long do I need to wait?'* Well, at long last, dear chums, the problem had a solution and it was not about destination displays at bus stops that give you the time of the next scheduled service (or not!). Oh no, don't even get me started on that particular hot potato.

It was about using clever cloud-based technology to deliver apps to customers and passengers so that they can rely on the information being accurate and sustainable or, to use another word, trustworthy.

Trains and planes have been using the technology accurately for a long time, but why have we been so slow to embrace the technology in the Bus and Coach Industry?

Well, I think that the problem is with people like me; as a typical middle-aged grumpy bloke, I have happily utterly ignored things like IT and the cloud because I don't really get it. Therefore, I ignore it and hope it will go away. But guess what – it does not and if you don't subscribe, then you miss out big time.

My Damascus moment came in 2009 when I was employed as the Commercial Manager for the Diamond Bus Company in Birmingham. It was a strong energetic team led by the charismatic Scott Dunn, a young, gifted, visionary MD. He gave the team the space we needed to experiment, and so we did and began, with a technology company, to track four buses on the 176 bus service from Redditch to Birmingham.

From the outset, for the first time, I could actually see what the drivers were doing. After 26 years of speculation, I had the answers and I thought to myself that this is the future, no more standing there not knowing if, or when, the bus might arrive.

The rest as they say is history, or should I say, uTrack!

On the Bus Live in Cork

So, there I was on the 261 bus from Cork Bus Station to the Jameson's distillery to see how God's own whiskey is brewed. I paid €9.90, not the €7.50 the website advertised and I'm was travelling on an elderly single decker, enjoying the beauty of the Irish coastline.

Try as I might I could not get the Wi-Fi to work, so I borrowed the good doctor's iPhone. There were 29 passengers on board enjoying the late autumn sunshine. As we stopped to let passengers off, the driver honked his horn at an old chap waving at the side of the road. You don't see that much in the UK, but to be fair life is more relaxed and friendly in Ireland. A lot of the passengers were using the Leap Card, which was actually good value for money.

The bus interior was very clean and, although knocking on a bit, the interior seats were pretty clean. The driver was swift, but not excessive in speed, and very soon we were in Middleton itself meandering down its main road before getting off right at the entrance to the distillery itself. Luckily for me the good doctor knew where to get off as the driver gave no information whatsoever for what must be one of Ireland's biggest tourist attractions.

I highly recommend the tours and, my word, what a mixed bag of people we were. We had Americans, French, Brazilians, Polish, Spanish, Germans, me – your token Englishman, and of course how could I forget the four Transylvanians!

At the end of the tour they asked for volunteers to become official whiskey tasters, after which you got a certificate with your name on it.

Luckily, the good doctor was aware of this, so we kept close to the guide, hoping to be in the frame. At the allotted point, I raised my hand casually to attract the tour guide's attention, only to be completely ignored, as I always am when waiting in bars.

Luckily for me, the good doctor was having none of it and with ruthless efficiency

Photo: Jackson Shaw on Unsplash

she managed to acquire the last remaining place at the tester table, which was duly given to me. Suffice to say I became the proud owner of a certificate, which was duly hung in a very appropriate place.

Happy days indeed, I felt grand!

And the Winners Are...
The Route One Awards!

I attended the excellent Route One Awards at the Hilton Metropole Hotel in downtown West Midlands. It was, by any stretch of the imagination, a lavish do, with the good and the great assembled in the rather splendid Monarch Suite of the Hilton. It was a busy night with not just one, but three, major awards ceremonies taking place.

Events kicked off with drinks at the bar for my guests as I welcomed them in and supplied their tickets (like a very posh, well-dressed, drug dealer, one friend pointed out) as I got the tickets out of a crumpled brown envelope, which I thought was slightly harsh if not mildly amusing.

Following that it was time to assemble for the pre-dinner drinks, which were served adjacent to the entrance of the Ballroom Suite where champagne and bottles of ice cold beer were the order of the day.

At 19:30 sharp, time was called and in we marched to join table 30, which enjoyed good views of the stage where the awards were to be presented to this year's winners. However, that was not until we had enjoyed the evening's rather fine food and wine, which included gammon hock or cheese tart for starters, followed by roast beef or vegetable Wellington for the main course. Interestingly enough, several guests misread the menu and went for beef Wellington, which sadly was not available (maybe it should have been as clearly there was a demand!).

In fairness, the food was very good with the cheesecake pudding disappearing from view very swiftly, as did the nice selection of Thorntons chocolates which accompanied the coffee and tea.

Then came the part we had all been waiting for as the winners were announced. There were 16 awards in total to be presented and the affair was well done as a double act between TV presenter and one time strictly contestant Katie Deerham and the affable editor of Route One, the main man himself, Mel Holley.

It was, as ever, an exciting night as winners were applauded and cheered more and more loudly as the wine flowed and beer was drunk.

The last award was a Lifetime Achievement Award presented to Stephen Barber, the Coaching Officer from the CPT. It was well deserved it after a lifetime of service to the industry.

The entertainment that followed was a comedian called Hal Cruttenden. I had seen him before on live at the Apollo, and thought that he was pretty good to be honest.

It was a tad unfortunate that his microphone was a bit muted as it was hard to hear, but he was actually very funny in my opinion.

However, the highlight of the night for me was when I was mistaken for the wine waiter by a chap that I have known for many years and hold in very high regard.

Indeed, had it not been for him many years ago, my whole Polish adventure would never have seen the light of day.

What happened was that the wine waiter, who was a very deaf, very old, Italian gentlemen who, quite honestly, used sign language as his means of communication, had momentarily left the wine menu at his portable table. I was then asked by one of my guests if I would select a bottle of Prosecco, so as I perused the menu, my friend came over and asked for two number 25s and a 31. At first I thought that he was having a laugh, so I joined in.

"Excellent sir, and which table number is it?" I said.

"Number 45," he replied and that was it, transaction done as far as he was concerned.

I had a dilemma, do I go along with it or do I point out that actually it was me and not the elderly deaf Italian wine waiter. So, as ever, honesty was the best policy, so I tapped him on the shoulder and asked him was he paying cash or card, he then looked at me in abject horror as he realised that he had mistaken me for Manuel.

I thought it was excellent sport, and before the night ended I made a point of asking him if I could get him anything else.

My good friend posted the trauma on Facebook, but mentioned no names, but the cat was out of the Route One Awards bag.

Greyhound Bus
A Legend

I remember when I was 21 years old I applied, and was successful, to go to the USA and get a job teaching Karate to young Americans. I had, in truth, no idea at all what I had let myself in for, but at the time it was exciting and a completely new adventure.

So, it was that I flew out on a chartered plane and found myself at the YMCA in downtown New York. By sheer coincidence a guy that I used to go to school with was also staying there, so he suggested we went to a bar that was owned by his uncle. Once there we were given free beer, which was a complete bonus, mostly because they all thought that we were Irish. Most people in my world think my

name is Burkes, which is an Irish name, actually Birks is an old English translation of Birchwood - just in case it pops up in a pub quiz.

So, it was that I found myself boarding a Greyhound bus to travel north across New York State to the middle of nowhere. I was, in fact, going to the Adirondack Mountains, to a place called Camp Saskatchewan. My experience was very interesting as the coach was pretty full.

What I observed was what I called real America, with all sorts of people riding the coach as it meandered around unknown towns and villages. Being curious I attempted to engage in conversation with those who spoke English, which was about 50% of the passengers.

Frankly it was quite hard work. I found elderly people most engaging, followed by college students. Each had their own stories to tell and it passed the time quite nicely. Some people had no idea I was British, indeed what I found quite amazing was just how little people knew of the UK, or indeed Europe.

However, as we drove on towards the six million acre park that is the Adirondack Mountains, some four hours north of New York City and only two hours away from Montreal, I realised that I was, up to a point, living the American dream and jumping on a Greyhound Bus to go and find work.

Strange to think that after all these years I would end up having shares in First Group, which bought Greyhound when my friend, David Leeder, was the man in charge of International Development back in 2006. It has had a troubled past, but today it looks better than ever.

Indeed, I am inspired to pop across the pond and take a road trip.

Hurrah.

Complaints...
Bad for the Soul

There are certain jobs in life that command, in my view, a natural respect from members of the great British public. One of which is those noble souls who, day in day out, man the phones or the laptops and deal with complaints.

It does not matter what the complaint is about, it is all about having to deal with the negative side of the human spirit.

I myself did this for a period of some three years. It was partly my own fault as at one of our monthly management meetings I had volunteered to do a review of the complaints analysis, and how we, as managers, handled them.

The results were interesting. The top four regular complaints were:

1. Late arrival;
2. Failing to stop and pick up passengers;
3. Early running; and
4. Driver attitude.

Probably few surprises there for those who run bus depots, but what was interesting was the different approaches made by different managers towards the whole culture of complaints.

Some were very good and professional, some were not. One especially was shocking. Every single complaint received the same two-line response, irrespective of the nature of what had happened. In fact, one passenger who had demanded a meeting with the MD (who sent me out to visit the lady at home) showed me seven identical letters she had received from this one chap that were utterly impersonal and disinterested. They actually made matters a lot worse as they sent such a negative and callous message. The replies were generic and although several complaints were about not running, one was an allegation that a driver had threatened her daughter, an extremely serious allegation treated with contempt and disdain and successfully pouring oil on troubled waters.

Clearly it was time for a review, so I ended up taking control for all the complaints. It was truly soul-destroying; all the phone calls came to me, one after the other. Apparently, it was because I had a depth of what HR types call *emotional intelligence*, I think the word that the other managers used was *mug*.

As far as they were concerned it was Christmas Day. No one likes dealing with these things, but if you make an effort it is possible to convert the negative into a positive.

I took all the calls and personally replied to every letter, making them personal to the individual. I also gave away lots of free day tickets which resulted in being awarded the nickname Austin *Day Rover enclosed* Birks.

At first I was handling 50 letters a day from the five depots and the only way to keep up was to take the damn things home at the weekend. This made it even worse, as that just took the misery home.

I soon realised that the only way to reduce them was to tackle the root cause. We targeted the biggest problem month-on-month and, bit-by-bit, reduced the volume.

After six months, the average daily total was down to 25, and, conversely, the volume of free tickets handed out went down. I kept them all the complaints and would occasionally recite them to my fellow workers just to try to cheer ourselves up.

And what lessons were learned? Well, quite simply, take complaints seriously, act quickly, apologise and reimburse where fair, and be human about it. Most people just want to sound off and have someone in authority be understanding and apologetic, and, of course, sending a reply always helps.

The Joy of Driving a Bus

Sometimes I have moments when I think back to how life was in the past and how life is now. There are, in truth, very few things that I regret. Indeed, overall, I think I have been pretty lucky in life.

However, sometimes I do find myself wistfully floating back through the mists of time to when I was lucky enough to spend six happy weeks driving my big, red, double-decker bus around the very beautiful countryside of West Yorkshire.

If you are not familiar with the land known locally as 'God's own county' it really is a very nice part of the UK and there is something very relaxing about just pottering about in a big red bus, on a bright, sunny autumnal day, with a large queue of irate motorists gently seething away behind you.

And, indeed, the look of pent-up frustration as you eventually pull over to allow them to

pass you by and acknowledge their friendly gestures with a jaunty smile and a wave back, all excellent practise for dealing with the Great British public, my very laid back instructor, Pete, used to say.

Indeed, he was so laid back that he used to go to the back of the bus, where he had virtually constructed a hammock, after a hearty lunch purchased from one of the excellent roadside cafes and caravans which he knew intimately. For example, he would proudly announce, *'Today is a Scotch Egg day'*, which was code for we are going towards Leeds and he knew a little cafe on a dual carriageway.

Or, and this was my personal favourite, *'Today is a Cornish pasty and mushy peas day',* this was a cheeky little trailer van on the outskirts of Hebden Bridge.

His logic was quite simple; once he felt that a student was competent to drive without his help, he would tell them where he wanted them to go, then retire to bed in his hammock.

I questioned him once on this somewhat dangerous approach and his reply was quite telling.

"Well son it's simple. I won't be out there to hold your hand when you pass your test and what is the difference between driving with a piece of paper and not driving with a piece of paper. I know myself when people are good enough to drive without me and by making them drive without me it builds up confidence, and that is what good driving is all about."

Sage words, but I am not sure that health and safety would quite see it that way had an accident taken place, which, to the best of my knowledge, it never did.

Ding ding, all aboard...

...the Festival Fun Coach
Care of National Express

I once (again) found myself in Digbeth Coach Station. As usual it was really busy, the usual collection of all sorts of people, ages, races, and creeds. To be honest I actually enjoy watching people come and go. It is not quite the pressure cooker of human emotions that you get at airports, when loved ones walk through the arrival doors to be greeted by those who have missed them so much. But it is, all the same, fascinating to watch the sea of mankind hopping on, and hopping off, the iconic branded National Express Coach.

However, on this particular day the coach station was jam packed full of young people, laden down with tents, sleeping bags, and kit as they were all bound in one direction, namely to Staffordshire and the V festival, where Jayzee was the headline act on the Saturday night and then Pink headlining on the Sunday. To be honest, those attending were dressed in a kaleidoscope of colours and styles that could probably be seen by the space station.

Obviously spirits were high and most looked like they were waiting for their GCSE results.

To be honest, tempers were in very high spirits as they drank their lattes and waited for their transport of delight, namely a good old National Express Coach. What was also interesting was that the vast majority indeed, actually every one of them come to think of it, had a smart phone and, of course, all being tech-savvy had, I have no doubt, downloaded the excellent Coach Tracker app so that they could monitor their progress.

Suitably inspired by the fact that NXC have been looking after gig attenders for so long, it got me thinking as to which other events NXC attend and, I have to say, it is an impressive coverage. Some events I have heard of and a lot I have not, but then again why would I. I do not think that late middle-aged English gentlemen fit the demographics of festivals.

However, these are the events that they cover, a massive 32 in all and quite varied they are as well: from Cheltenham Festival to Wembley; Fusion; Wilderness; Green Man; Twickenham; V Festival; Glastonbury; Leeds; Reading; Global Gathering; Latitude; MK Bowl; Sonisphere; Grand National; City of Manchester Stadium; NEC; Royal Ascot; Boomtown Fair; Download Festival; Olympic Stadium; End of the Road; Victorious Festival; Y Not Festival; El Dorado Festival; T in the Park; Southbeats Festival; Electric Daisy Carnival; Wembley Arenas; and finally, and most appropriately, the last one, Sundown Festival.

So, as they say, something for everyone. Quite literally, all tastes catered for from old to young, and that, in all fairness, sums up National Express.

All things to all men and women and children which, after all, is the definition of the word *omnibus*, a perfect ending.

Watch Out For Your Hampton Court

I was very fortunate to have a conversation with an excellent chap who I used to work with at my days at First in the Midlands. I first met Steve Zanker when First in the Midlands Bus Company merged with First Leicester and Northampton, when my mate, Big Ken Mills, decided it was time to get out the deck chair and hang up his hat.

The first thing that I noticed was that Steve not only had a very sharp sense of humour, but he used to keep a dice in his pocket. However, instead of having numbers it simply had the word 'maybe' printed on all sides. I was always intrigued as to why he carried this around and in fact to this day I have no idea.

I think that I hoped that it was when we were in discussions with the brothers from the trades unions, and when they asked for an increase in salary he would say let's roll the dice... maybe.

Anyway, on one occasion we were invited to a public meeting in a place called Hampton Dene in Hereford. Long story short, we reduced the frequency of the buses and cut the evening services as the route was losing money. As it happened the local ward councillor was up for re-election so was handed a cause celeb on a plate.

As we drove into the car park, we could see that the hall was jam-packed with people who were clearly not happy.

"Oh dear, this could turn ugly," I said to Steve, trying to look suitably serious as we shuffled in and made our way to the front. Silence descended on the mob, as the main course was offered to the baying brood.

The councillor stood up and requested quiet.

"Right, this is Mr Birks, who some of you remember from before (*a few boos...*) and this is Mr Zanker who has come from Leicester. They have come to explain themselves."

At that point an elderly lady could not hold back, "It's a disgrace, you two should be ashamed of yourselves." (*much clapping and encouragement this only served to wind her up even more*). "And one day, you will be old."

Suddenly she appeared to stop in mid-sentence as the horror unfurled.

The poor woman had got herself into such a state of frenzy that her false teeth had managed to separate from the safe home of her mouth. It was almost as if they were still chattering as she vainly tried to catch them in mid-flight. For some reason I was momentarily reminded of geese.

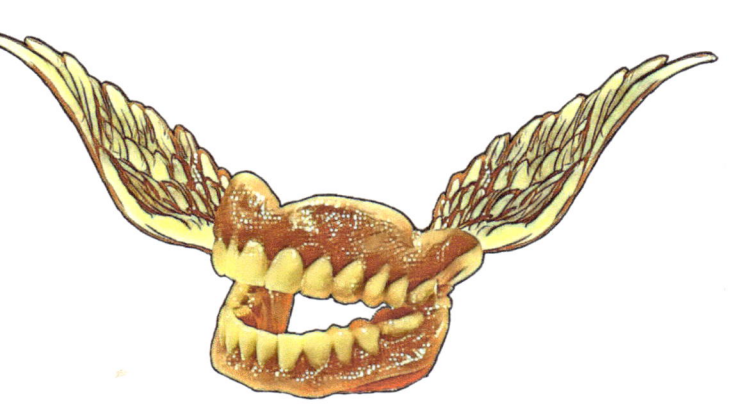

Eventually some semblance of order did return, and I stood up and announced that we at the company fully understood that it was an emotive issue and that bus services are the lifeline of the community.

However, following 1986, they were also commercial services and the route at Hampton Court was losing money. A strange noise broke out behind me as I could hear giggling. When I turned round, Steve was desperately trying not to laugh and failing, the shoulders were going up and down and try as he might he could not control himself.

At which point the councillor stood up and said, "Well Mr. Birks, you might think it's funny but let me remind you this is Hampton Dene, It is definitely not Hampton Court, that is something very different, let me tell you."

We did not stay long; I was in a state of shock for days.

Fetch the Wheelbarrow
We Are Off to the Bank

Do you ever have one of those moments when you think back over the years at things that you may have done that in today's *PC/Health and Safety* world would be utterly forbidden? Yes? No?

Well, either way I am going to regale you with something that happened that, even as I write it, I actually question myself that it actually happened. But yes it did.

You have to go back through the mists of time to 1988. There I was, the young, fresh-faced Manager of Hereford Depot. Things were going well. I had been there for a year or so and was cutting my teeth bit by bit.

We had recently launched our fleet of |Hereford Hoppers and the money was rolling in quite nicely for various reasons, but one was definitely that creative fare table management! Anyway, all was tickety boo, we had a nice routine and a great team. As my dad used to say, everything in the garden was lovely.

However, the peace was shattered at 04:59 one Thursday morning when I got a call from my right-hand man, Howard, who was always the first to get to the depot.

"Hello?" I said, more asleep than awake, "Who is it?"

"It's me gaffer. You need to get down here, the safe has gone, the place is an absolute tip?"

"The safe gone?" I replied, not really taking this in. It was a big safe.

"Yes," he said, "hook, line and sinker. The Police are on the way."

So that was it. Off I popped and when I got there it was a scene of devastation. The whole office had been wrecked. Clearly these boys knew what they were doing; proper professionals. So I liaised with head office and the Police, as scenes of crimes were all over it, as this was a pro job. Slowly, but surely, we began to work around the mess and tried to restore some semblance of order.

At about midday I called a team meeting and we planned what we were going to do with the takings, as the money was starting to come in as the early shifts began to return and, of course, there was no safe. So where do we put the cash?

Ken Mattey, right-hand man number two, suggested that we needed, in the absence of a safe, to talk to a local bank to see if we could make a temporary arrangement. Ken helpfully suggested that the manager of Nationwide Bank, located in the centre of the City, was an old drinking chum and no doubt would be delighted to help.

Two hours later, Len returned having enjoyed a liquid lunch with his friend and advised me that they now had a plan.

"Excellent," I said, "what are we going to do?"

"Well," he said, "as the money comes in, we

Looks Like We Got Us a Convoy!

will bag it up and then at 11:00 pm tonight, with a Police escort, we will wheel the money to the bank where the manager has arranged for a staff member to receive it and keep it safe."

Silence descended. Giggling was close to the surface.

"So, let me get this straight. I get that we bag it up etc. all – that is fine, but why can't we just put it in a van and drive up there?"

"Because it is pedestrianised now, and you can't drive," he replied. "Don't worry, there will be three Police officers with us, so we will have a convoy."

So, that was what we did. I told head office who advised that it would take three days to replace the safe. No one questioned it, as far as they were concerned it was a solution. So, at 11:00 pm, having enjoyed several convivial hours in the Military club located next door, we had ourselves a convoy. Mattey led the charge, with barrow number one, me in the middle, with barrow number two and right-hand man bringing up the rear. We had two Police officers at the front and two at the back. Our ETA we reckoned was eight minutes, as Mattey had taken it upon himself to do a dummy run.

Two issues emerged. First, when he went the barrow was empty. Second, we had all had about five pints of Marston's Pedigree finest bitter, and did not realise how heavy six grand was in three wheelbarrows, and, when you are reasonably inebriated, the actual arrival time took 20 minutes.

So, it happened that we got there and drove our barrows in. A nice man took control, gave us receipts as all the money was bagged, and off we went back to the depot with our convoy. This went on for three nights until the new safe arrived.

When I think of today's world and what would have happened had we replicated the process, I suspect that we would have been summarily dismissed on the spot. But back in the day it was a very different world where what really mattered was the solution not the execution.

Happy Days!

Industrial Tribunals
The Importance of Getting it Right

Once upon a life when I was based at Leeds, in deepest darkest Yorkshire, I was told that I had to attend an industrial tribunal. I had not been to one before and in truth I was not sure what to expect. So, I turn up at the depot with the District Traffic Superintendent (DTS) whose name was Brian, he was a nice enough, affable sort of chap, who, like me, had absolutely no idea what he was about to let himself in for.

So, we trundled off to a large council office where the play was about to be performed. I casually asked what the background was and Brian informed me that he had dismissed a driver for theft, he was also the senior shop steward. Oh, I thought, that could be lively. So, when we arrive a chap comes up, introduces himself as the company lawyer and gave a quick resume of what the plan was. He would explain to the three members of the industrial tribunal team the background to the case and the reasons for the dismissal.

What would happen then was that the trades union's lawyers (three of them!) would then put the case for unfair dismissal. After that, any persons required to give evidence would be brought in, sworn in on the Good Book and prepare to bat before being cross-examined.

Excellent wheeze I thought, this could be fun. So, in we all troop and to my surprise the place is nearly full, it was like a proper court with a public gallery, the press were there, the only people missing were the paparazzi. Suddenly, I felt decidedly uncomfortable as did Brian who looked a bit white.

So, the three judges came in, we all stand, like you do in the crown court, and then we sat down. Introductions were given and our chap kicked off.

He explained that the driver, Mr X, had been checked by a bus inspector where three passengers had been given tickets that had been issued the day before. All the passengers confirmed that the driver had taken their money and gave them the tickets. The tickets could only have been given by the driver and none of the passengers had seen the driver print out the tickets from his ticket machine. He had simply given them a ticket from his tray. This meant of course that he had deliberately picked up old tickets and handed them out. Bang to rights you would think.

In line with company procedure, the driver was immediately suspended and taken back to the depot where he was formally suspended pending a formal disciplinary interview with the DTS at 09:00 the next morning. Now, because he was the senior shop steward he

was entitled to the full-time officer to be present, so the guy is duly called up.

The interview took place the next day. Nice Brian got him in, went through the facts and then asked for an explanation. The driver refused to reply to the charges. So, nice Brian said that considering the facts; three customers all saying the same thing that pre-issued tickets had been given, in his opinion he was guilty and so would be summarily dismissed from company service with immediate effect.

So, with that our chap sat down and then the first of the trades union's chaps stood up. He then says that clearly his man denied all charges and said that there was clearly an error with the ticket machine which had issued incorrect tickets. Stunned disbelief from me and Brian. So, then he asked to cross-examine, a nervous, Brian.

Up he got into the dock and the lawyer said, "Did you check the ticket machine?"

"No," replied nervous Brian, "at no stage did the driver suggest that there was a problem, he just refused to comment."

"So," asked the lawyer, "would it be possible to have the ticket machine examined to see if there was any problem with it?"

"I suppose so," Brian stuttered.

At that point he went away to arrange to get the required ticket machine and records checked. An hour goes by when he reappeared ashen-faced and informed me and the brief that it has disappeared.

Brian was now very worried as he informed the tribunal that it couldn't be found, so having been put in a very awkward position the tribunal decided that they needed to adjourn to consider what next to do.

So, one hour later they come back in and the Chairman starts. "We have a very unusual situation on our hands here. In the absence of the ticket machine and without proper records to check the claim by the driver we cannot, in fairness, uphold the decision to dismiss him. He is, therefore, to be reinstated with immediate effect and have any loss of pay reimbursed with immediate effect."

Nice Brian was devastated Brian at the enormity of having to pay back four months' pay as well as everything else that went with it. I did not know what to say, so I said nothing.

The ticket machine, strangely, was never found. As a result, shortly after, nice Brian became retired early Brian. And I learned all about making sure that you cover all angles because tribunals are as much about correct procedure as they are about delivering just and fair decisions.

Riverdance In West Bromwich Bus Station

You might recall a TV advert from a few years ago that showed what appeared to be a random mob who assemble at a London railway station and spontaneously break out in a series of dances, much to the amusement and joy of ordinary members of the public, some of whom joined in.

In truth, it was an extremely clever and well-rehearsed piece of advertising on behalf of a major mobile telephone company. Indeed, it got me thinking as to what we in the bus and coach industry could do about marketing our services. How did we compare to some of the heavyweights in the UK marketing stakes?

I remember very little in terms of TV advertising. In fairness, First did well with their regional TV advert campaign, it's fair to say that it was not high tech and seemed to focus on involving staff members singing a jolly song, extolling the virtues of working for First.

Some 30 years ago, National Express launched a major TV campaign that involved Beeper, the talking cartoon frog, who was promoting the new livery of National Express coaches and the super new fleet of double-decker coaches along with the attractive lady hostesses who were blatantly copied from the airlines. Well, did it work? Clearly it did as some 30 odd years on I still remember it. Surprising as usually I can't remember what happened yesterday.

It is interesting to contrast the rail industry's approach to advertising compared to bus and coach. Most adverts focus on ticketing and pricing (come on and compare the train line!). Ghastly, cheesy, but I still remember it, annoying as it may be. But, as for the bus and coach, there's very little evidence of large-scale spending that I can recall. And what about radio adverts? Do they work? How can you actually tell if your advert works? I

have long been a believer in the benefit of local radio adverts, but they need to be quirky and sharp to be effective. But what do today's large players think about the benefit (or not) of volume corporate advertising? I can't answer that, but what I do know is that clever and different adverts like the flash mob at the station are worth a lot, which takes me back to my plan to re-create Riverdance in West Bromwich Bus Station.

I had it all planned; at around 16:30, a single Diamond Bus Driver would stand in the middle of the exit in the bus station and start Michael Flatley's famous routine as the music starts to blare around the bemused, Black Country folk. A single lady bus driver arrives from the opposite side, and suddenly, the tempo gathers pace as, from left and right, more bus drivers emerge to swell the orchestrated ranks of Riverdancers all letting the joy flow to the mirth and amusement of all assembled.

I actually did a fair bit of prep for this, signing up drivers, fitters, cleaners, managers, etc. I even got initial permission from Centro who manage the bus stations, and good enthusiastic support from those in charge.

All was seemingly going well, until...

I am sure you can guess who got involved and put the kibosh on the whole darn thing. Yes, it had to be, it could only be the good folk from Health and Safety, who decreed that performing Riverdance in West Bromwich Bus Station was *a significant health and safety risk to the members of the general public, as well as to the welfare of the dancing drivers.*

It was not until sometime after I had left the company that I was informed that said Health and Safety Executive had not been told that the bus station would, in fact, be shut down specially for the duration of the performance and had thought that the whole thing would take place with buses operating as usual.

Sometimes, these people beggar belief.

Photograph by Tony Hisgett - Flickr: Bus Station, CC BY 2.0, https://commons.wikimedia.org/w/index.php?curid=15806231

The Beautiful Game

Some time ago, I was reminded of the annual five-a-side football competition that we used to organise back in the days of Midland Red West in the 80s. Every year, various teams representing the seven different depots would turn up to play 'Kick the Manager'.

My first experience was a baptism of fire. It was held on a cold, November, Sunday morning, and I was playing for the Head Office team as all managers were told that they were not allowed to play for their personal depots because we were *'management'*. Having always played and loved football, I had done the decent thing on the Saturday and left the beer out, thinking that I needed a clear head and athletic limbs.

So, I duly turned up at a large leisure centre in Redditch, parked the car and wandered in. Milling about were loads of people, most of whom I did not recognise. I then spotted our MD, Ken Mills, who pointed out where the managers were and joined in the banter while we got changed.

I looked at the team sheet; we were the Heron Lodgers since we worked at the head office called Heron Lodge, fair enough. My own lads from Hereford were *The Hereford Heroes*, *The Worcester Warriors* (which set the tone for their style of play), *The Redditch Ruffians* (clearly a pattern developing here), *The Evesham Heffers* (very rural and judging from the monster beer bellies on display, quite descriptive), *The Kidderminster Kamikazes* (not that anyone was Japanese), and last, but certainly not least, *The Birmingham Zulus*.

I was somewhat surprised at why they called themselves the Zulus, so I asked one of my management chums and he said that at Birmingham City football club, the most notorious football hooligans are called the Zulus as they have a ferocious reputation across the land.

"Oh," I said, "So did they named themselves in tribute to the Zulus?"

"No, they are the Zulus," he said.

OMG!

And as they sauntered off the coach that unloaded them, I could see that he was not joking. They were almost all completely legless before they got changed. The main man was called Tank, I believe that he was christened Sherman, but as far as I was concerned, he could call himself anything he liked.

Well, eventually the football, or what passed for it, began. What swiftly became apparent was that whenever the management played, the ball was not required. It was horrendous, and with more alcohol being consumed throughout the course of the morning and afternoon, it became extremely intense. I soon discovered that my best strategy was to try to avoid any contact with the ball, completely at odds to all my natural instincts.

On occasions, it was a bit like the hockey games from the classic St. Trinian's films, except without the hockey sticks. At any given time, hand-to-hand combat was required as scores were settled, and good old healthy tribal differences literally kicked in.

The icing on the cake was the final which saw the Zulus take the Ruffians apart. It was a mismatch from the start with the Zulus enjoying a style of football that resembled Eric Cantona's classic Kung Fu exploits with fans. The referees were helpless and were equally intimidated, and the Zulus, now drunker than ever, walked away with the cup. In fact, they were about the only ones who could walk at all.

Happy days looking back.

And as Ken used to say, "Good to see the lads letting off a bit of steam."

Always the master of the understatement.

Bus Driver Training

When you consider the Bus Industry in the UK, the one area that never really made that much sense to me was how the sausage machine was focused on churning out people who could pass the PCV test. And then, depending on the degree of driver shortage, the hapless individual was given, at best, the minimum route learning and deposited out on the streets, often underprepared and overwhelmed.

In addition, the circus became more bizarre when they were immediately subjected to the rigours of the disciplinary code, irrespective of how under experienced they were.

The result: a remarkably high churn of people who were either sacked quickly or, quite frankly, could not stand the alien culture and unsympathetic rigidity of the system, and just for good measure, let's not forget the good old-fashioned top dog culture.

This normally resulted in long-serving and, although not necessarily any good, drivers having their own section in the canteen (enter at your peril!) as well as first pick of the best buses and the best, easiest routes. It was great for those with such an exalted status, but a nightmare of confusion, and sometimes even bullying, for the new, the shy and vulnerable.

The worst elements of that behaviour were in stark contrast to the changing customer-facing training that was taking the retail trade by storm.

And I just sincerely hope that today's modern bus business understands the key importance of looking after the individual. Of course, driving skills are paramount, but it is the support and nurture levels that actually really create a loyal, motivated employee, which is the best asset that any company will ever have!

Technology in the Bus and Coach Industry

Harold Wilson, a onetime Prime Minister of this great nation, once famously said, *'A week is a long time in politics'* – a clever saying from a clever man.

Back in the day, he was also reportedly to have been one of the Queen's favourite Prime Ministers from the 13 or so that she has had to work with, including stable and strong Theresa, or weak and wobbly Mrs May, depending on which newspaper that you want to read.

The reason I mention this is simple. When I joined the industry back in 1066 or to be more accurate 1983, it was only just beginning to embrace the new-found technology of computers. Indeed, I had a summer job in 1978 on what was then called the Viable Network Project or VNP as it was lovingly known. This basically required an army of people riding round on numerous buses on the Midland Red network, which back then was enormous, interviewing thousands of bus passengers.

My temporary job was to basically ensure that the thousands of forms that the passengers filled in were then read by a computer that was simply huge. The machine then processed the raw data and then drew conclusions. The logic behind all this was simple; the company wanted to redesign the operating network, so they could operate networks that reflected modern passenger needs. The processing of all these million bits of information required a small army of part-time people like me and another army of full-time people.

Looking back to the world then compared to the world now I cannot believe just how slow the industry has been. When I think back to the VNP project, it was actually innovative and cutting edge, but from then until probably the middle of 2005 not an awful lot more seemed to take place that I can recall. I am sure things came and went, but nothing really earth shattering happened until the last ten years or so when there was a sudden and dramatic explosion of technology.

How do I know? Well because I have been fortunate enough to witness it all myself, up close and personal, not just with the amazing technology of uTrack, but across multiple platforms. From the alcolock alcohol tester to driver standard scoring systems, like Green Road, Traffilog, and Mix Telematics. These and numerous other clever and smart technologies have transformed this industry and it is really only just starting. As the world's first driverless buses started to roll out, and the world of disruptive technology gained greater momentum, it posed big questions across the spectrum of the Bus and Coach Industry.

However, I honestly believed that this would only make the industry better and, more importantly, of greater social value than ever before.

On the positive side it was encouraging

to see that the Mayor of London, introduced plans to put the bus at the heart of the public transport strategy.

So just what will the next ten years bring? Time will tell, but the internet of everything is escalating rapidly, a new world or driverless vehicles with alternative power sources can only be imagined.

Nostalgia
Ain't What it Used to Be

I once stumbled upon a post on Facebook from an old mate from the days when I worked for First in the Midlands, or Midland Red West as it used to be called.

It was a newspaper article about an old bus depot in Bromsgrove with a rather sad, black and white photo of the large depot; its factual information, basically saying that the site was now up for sale.

Thirty years on, the message was where did those 30 years go? And clearly, I am now getting seriously old, because I realised that I have no idea where the years have gone. One minute I was young and then I woke up and suddenly I was not young anymore.

I know it's a cliché, but it is very true, time flies. Of course, it does not really, it is just the perception of time that changes. To put this is context, I rang a call centre about a broadband provider. I rang an 0800 number and spoke to a very nice man who lived elsewhere.

In a nutshell, I spent 45 minutes of my life that completely dragged. The minutes seemed to last an eternity as I was put on hold repeatedly, unable to do anything else as one supervisor after another told me that on checking the system it was clearly OK.

So, what was my problem?

My problem was no blasted broadband connection. I found my grumpy middle-aged man button being repeatedly pressed by an army of people who clearly lacked any aspiration for excellent customer service. I watched the clock which not only stopped, but started to go backwards, such was my exasperation at the pointless circle of people I had to talk to.

But fast forward to today and I can recall the first time that I ever set foot at Midland Red West and meeting the nice man who put the post on Facebook. He told me how sad he was that he had not only lost his depot and place of work, he had lost his community; his *tribe* was the word he used.

I know exactly what he meant. I felt the same way when I left my depot at Hereford. I had invested seven years of my life building my depot, with my people. That was how I felt, and I still do. Happy days I recall, but they, of course, had the bad and sad moments as life has; it's all part of the journey.

The trouble is that one day, out the blue, you have a Damascus moment when you realise that your journey is not exactly over, but let's put it this way, on the escalator of life you are well and truly past half way. Nothing to panic about, just need to get the most of the days or years that lie ahead.

Nibbles the Hamster
The Power of the Media

So, there I was minding my own business on a quiet Friday afternoon when I received a phone call from my good friend, Ian Humphreys, the extremely capable MD of First in the Midlands Bus Company. "Austin, can you pop into the office? We have a problem."

So, off I popped to find Ian and my other good chum, Steve Zanker, the Commercial Director, looking a tad perplexed, and I said,

So, to quote the Guardian newspaper as reported on Saturday 24th August 2002:

'A hamster at the centre of cash for travel row has been awarded a free travel pass. The bus Company, First Northampton apologised to the pair for the top-up charge yesterday, awarding Jordan free bus travel for a month and giving Nibbles his own lifetime travel pass.

The pair was then given a trip around the town on one of the Company's buses with the destination saying, 'The Hamster Special'.

Austin Birks, a spokesman for the Company apologised to the pair and thanked them for drawing attention to a gap in the firms' travel policy.

He said: "We realised that we had no policy for hamster travel, so we have released the first ever guidelines for hamsters using our buses.

First, hamsters are encouraged to travel free of charge on any of our services, preferably accompanied by a fare-paying human.

Secondly, young hamsters will be asked to give up their seat to an elderly or infirm hamster.

Thirdly, we request young hamsters do not use mobile phones or Walkmans while travelling on our buses for the comfort and convenience of other hamsters."

"What appears to be the problem?"

Ian replied, "We have a bit of a situation in Northampton. It seems that one of our drivers has charged a 10-year-old boy 10 pence to take his hamster, Nibbles, on one of our buses. The boy's mum has rung the local paper and, as a result, Radio 5 have picked up on it and are now asking for an interview with a Company spokesperson, which is where you come in."

Pause... think, then giggling broke out... well, there is only one thing for it, we need to turn this on its head and create a Hamster policy and give the boy the required apology and a gesture of goodwill.

Well, all hell broke loose... I did scores of radio interviews and it went global. BBC TV appeared, and I did lots of interviews, the Sun even did a cartoon. I received in excess of 70 emails from around the world – from Russia to Canada; it seemed to capture the media's attention.

In truth, you can't make this stuff up. It put us on the map and it generated a great deal of positive publicity, when really, it was just a mistake by a bus driver. Any other day it would have quietly slipped past, but it did not, and to this day, I still have an email from someone in Russia who applauded the actions on behalf of the International Hamster League.

The key point is how thinking out of the box can create a huge tsunami from a tiny ripple...

Now That is What I Call Initiative!

I was extremely amused to read of a bus driver in Preston who was arrested as he had successfully managed to sell the bus he was driving to a nice gentleman called Mr Yusef Aslem, a millionaire from Dubai who he'd got into conversation with.

The driver managed to sell the bus, which he claimed was his, to the gentleman who agreed to pay him £14,000 for the bus which, when he got the bus back to his native land, he was going to convert to a mobile restaurant.

Now to be honest I do not know where to start with this. If I did not know different I would think that it was April 1st.

First, what was an Arab millionaire doing on a bus, and in Preston?

Second what inspired the driver to think that he could actually get away with it? I have to, dare I say it, admire the sheer balls of the bloke for selling the bus. It showed some commercial acumen that many employed in such positions have failed to show.

There was a real spirit of entrepreneurship amongst some of my bus driver friends that I have observed in my long career in the Bus and Coach Industry. The only trouble is, that very often it was directed against the companies they worked for and was actually theft. Now, some took the view it was a bit of additional pocket money that bought a cup of tea now and again. Others I met took an almost industrial view, and tackled the challenge with gusto.

One case, quite early on in my career, was in Bootle in Merseyside where four drivers had combined their talents and had actually managed to get hold of their own private ticket machines. Looking back it was a very well thought-out operation. They would take it in turns to sneak their own ticket machine on the bus and then, part way through the journey, would start issuing kosher tickets with the company's own ticket rolls. It was genius in its simplicity as *all* the tickets issued were the same. Any inspector checking tickets would see nothing wrong. The only difference being that all the money went straight to the drivers.

Of course they ended up getting greedy and eventually one of their fellow bus drivers blew the whistle. The Police were involved, dawn raids took place and all four were given suspended prison sentences that validated the old adage that actually crime does pay. Mind you, I suppose it is a narrow line to cross.

When I was the Depot Manager for Hereford back in my youth, I took an executive decision to put the fares up and not tell anyone. As a result we started, as a depot, to make some very good money, way ahead of budget. At the monthly senior management meetings the boss, Big Ken Mills, would say, *'Well young'un you have done it again, a great performance, much better than budget'.*

Now of course I knew the answer to my dark secret and the better it got the longer I rode the wave. And then, crash! I got found out by accident.

I was summoned on a Monday morning to Head Office where the MD, Finance Director, and Engineering Director gave a dressing down the likes of which I had never experienced before.

I thought I'd get the sack as I had broken their trust, but I had made the company a shed load of money and opinion was split.

Suffice to say, I lived to fight another day and learned my lesson. Some said I got away with it, and I suppose that I did, but I never made a single penny from my wrong doing, just a lot of money for my depot and company.

Mind you, at least I never sold any of our buses to Arabian millionaires.

Although come to think of it...

Commonwealth Games
Utrack – a Driving Force

Photo by Phil Reid on Unsplash

I had to go to Glasgow to meet an old friend of mine and talk about possibly uTrack doing some tracking for the friend's buses for the Commonwealth Games that were due to be staged across the fair cities of Glasgow and Edinburgh.

I'd experienced just how good they were when I went to Dorchester to witness the sailing and my experience of using the Park and Ride service was quite simply excellent. So, naturally, expectations were suitably high for a smooth operation in Scotland where the world's attention would be focused on the delivery of an excellent and seamless Games.

However, the truth was that these events do not just happen, they require pristine planning and attention to detail, and the First Games delivery team had been working solidly with a massive range of partners to ensure that everybody got to where they needed to be, on time, every time.

I was amazed at the sheer complexity of it all and, in truth, I really don't think that I could have handled the massive pressure and responsibility that this attracts. But fortunately, there was a really good team managing that monster job. Andy Scholey, the director responsible, his right-hand man, Andy Hunter, the Operations Director, Richard Kirk, Lee Wright, these guys were the real heroes to me.

Yes, of course, the athletes would be the stars of the show, but we also needed to appreciate that there was a small army of people who would not appear on podiums or get medals, but we should not forget their contribution. And despite all the logistical and practical challenges that needed to be overcome by so many different organisations at the end of the day, just like the Olympics, the Commonwealth Games would be judged on how smoothly they work.

uTrack were selected to provide all the tracking for all of the vehicles that would provide the transport for those taking part in and organising the Commonwealth Games. The job of delivering the right people, to the right place, at the right time had fallen to the excellent team at First Games Transport team who had already done a truly amazing job during the 2012 Olympics.

This was a large event and the eyes of the world would be firmly fixed on Glasgow and Edinburgh as they hosted competitors from over 60 countries within the Commonwealth. These included superstars like Usain Bolt and Mo Farah, so it was absolutely essential they were transported safely and smoothly.

The responsibility was split between over 30 different bus and coach companies, most of whom had different telematics providers. The challenge for uTrack was to make sure that the systems were all compatible and that the tracking would be seamless. This required each vehicle to be fitted with a box, or another device, that could transmit a satellite location every 30 seconds so giving a GPS data source.

There were a number of operators that had well-appointed telematics providers, such as Mix Telematics and Traffilog, others, however, did not, so they needed to be fitted quickly as the Games were approaching rapidly. And there were the economies of scale that needed to be addressed as companies with less than five vehicles could be as problematic as larger fleets.

However, the key to success was clear organisation and strong project management, and those elements were being implemented. But we were under no illusions that it would be a great challenge for a project that would last no longer than three weeks, and we did our best to deliver.

So, as they used to say after the Second World War, *'What did you do in the War Daddy?'*

Well, what uTrack did was to take telematics feeds from over 30 different companies with a daily PVR of, on the busiest day, 536 buses and coaches, and track them to ensure they were generally at the right time and place they were supposed to be. That meant that if a driver was off route then he could be put back on the right route. It also highlighted where the low bridges were, so avoiding calamity.

The other big help was historic reporting, so when complaints were made, they could investigate accordingly and either uphold or defend said complaint. It is always inevitable that drivers, being human, would make mistakes and get lost. The clever thing was to have the technology in place that allowed for swift corrections to take place.

It was a massive challenge to be overcome with the closing ceremony when a lot of coaches needed to be at one very small place at the same time. Still, if there is one thing that First Games enjoy that is a challenge, and they certainly rose to that.

As I watched the telly as one sport after another was exhibited and gold medals were dished out, and with England and Scotland doing exceptionally well, the Games were celebrated, quite rightly, as an overwhelming success.

Best of all, uTrack played its role in ensuring part of the logistics success.

Mutt and Geoff...
...and Misheard Words

Life has a strangeness about it that is sometimes genuinely hard to understand. Also, oddly my rather strange sense of humour may also cloud my own personal judgement. I am one of those people who can see the sublime and the ridiculous in the most bizarre situations. Indeed, dear reader, you may well have noticed this yourself.

Sometimes I genuinely just sit down and start writing and the strangest memories, and indeed exaggerations, conspire to make me laugh to the point of tears. It is really odd how these mental images just appear as if by magic. However, sometimes things happen that are just genuinely funny. The sort of thing that just happens, no one planned it, it just naturally occurs.

One such event happened when Conor, the uTrack IT Director, and I went to Derby to visit the Depot Manager, a very nice man called Geoff. He was on the brink of retirement and had spent his life in the Bus Industry. We met quite a lot of people at the meeting and Conor explained how uTrack worked and what we required in terms of timetable and stop information.

Most of the eight or so people at the meeting were planners, mostly men with beards in their 50s and a very high degree of cynicism towards technology and indeed the whole cloud-based world.

Conor, as ever, was professional and competent as he tried to allay their fears as to what this dark magic could actually do. One chap was especially challenging and took the view of 'yes I have seen and heard all this before and it never works'.

At that point, Conor got out his iPhone and showed them the Dublin Coach app that demonstrated exactly what uTrack was able to do. The result was a stunned silence as somehow the dark magic seemed to do exactly what it said on the tin.

At that point, Geoff said, "Well, that is marvellous, I honestly do not understand what you just showed me, but I am sure that it will be very good and I am looking forward to my retirement."

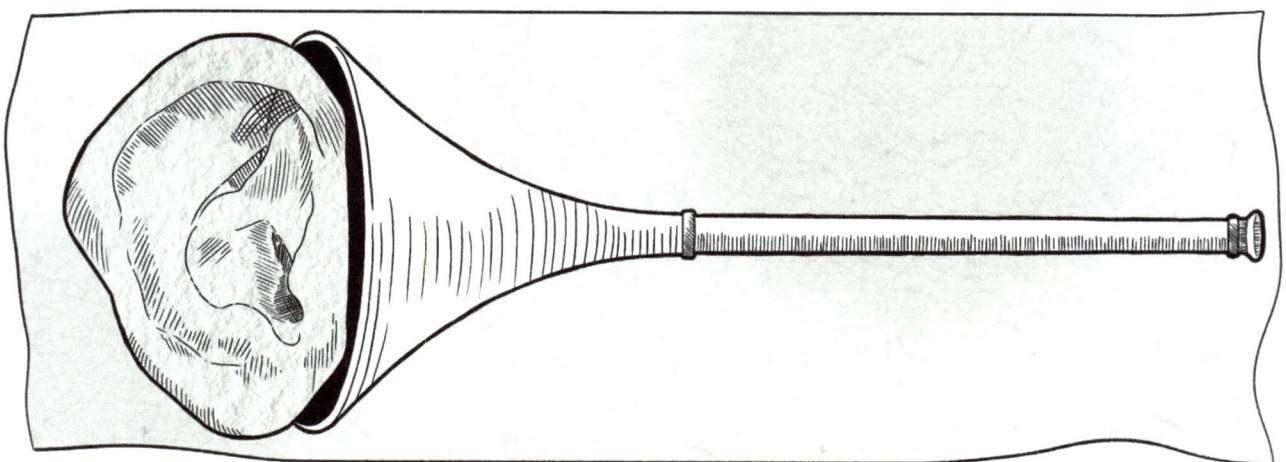

Heads nodding all around, Conor then said, "Right, well, if you do not mind it would be good to go out on the routes and have a look around."

All of a sudden Geoff became very animated and said, "Oh no, that is far too dangerous. We could not possibly let you do that, I could not guarantee your security or safety."

Conor and I stand there looking at him utterly bewildered, and then the penny dropped.

"No Geoff," said Conor, "we do not want to go on the roof, we want to go on the routes."

Giggling then broke out amongst all concerned as a very embarrassed Geoff tried to explain that because uTrack worked with satellites, somehow, we would pop onto the roof and send one up, as you do when dealing with cloud-based technology.

I never leave home without sending up a satellite, I mean that is what you do is not it? Well no actually it's not. Misunderstanding is a joy to behold.

As for Geoff, he retired shortly afterwards. God bless him.

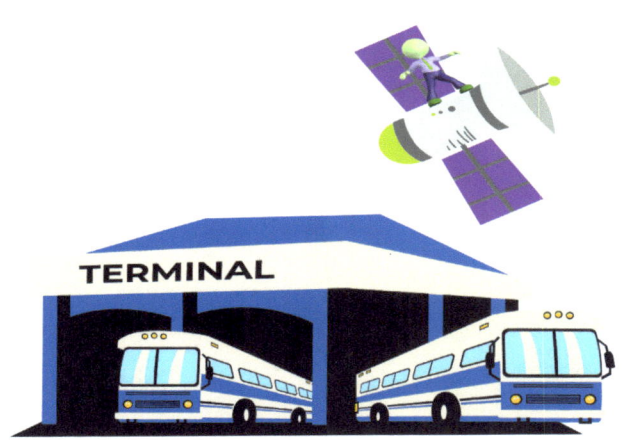

May The Forth Be With You

Always been a Star Wars fan me, don't know why. Perhaps it goes back to my childhood love of watching Doctor Who as a young boy, back in the days of black and white TV, and large family-sized sofas behind which you could hide.

When I look back at Doctor Who then compared to now I can't believe what a huge difference there is. True, some things I am delighted to say remain constant like Daleks and Cybermen, for example, Daleks these days can even go upstairs, which they did not used to able to do. It was easy to escape a pursuing Dalek back then, all the good Doctor had to do was leg it up the stairs or climb a tree. Simples.

However, from the swinging '60s to today's world, life is virtually unrecognisable and consequently, people and passengers' expectations are radically different now. Back in the 60s when I went to school, all buses had bus conductors I think that Boris had plans to employ bus conductors in the future in London, although they would be more like fielders in cricket whose job it would be to catch passengers as they fell out of the back of the bus where there is a big hole. Howzat!

Passengers, or customers as I like to call them, expect certain basic commodities that back in the '60s would have been viewed as pure science fiction, much in the same way as Star Wars and Doctor Who.

Coach Tracker 2
Revolutionising National Express Coach Company

Today's punter wants things like Wi-Fi, leather seats, low floor access, wheelchair and buggy space. Oh yes, the list goes on, and why not? The bus industry is a retail business that needs to be aware of customer expectations and respond accordingly. And so the industry should promote today's technology as a means of attracting middle-class car users onto buses and public transport. There is growing evidence that people are choosing the bus because they can access Wi-Fi. A good example is my daughter who has a one-hour ten-minute bus journey to college and back so it is ideal to do homework or revision etc.

All extremely fine and dandy, but as a note of caution if promoting the values of Wi-Fi, just make sure that you can guarantee that there is actually coverage available on the network. One operator scored an own goal when, having promoted the benefits and whetted the appetite of the customers, when it actually went live within eight minutes of starting the journey the network coverage stopped and so did the Wi-Fi... Time for a Homer Simpson style Doh!

Sadly in this case the force was definitely not with them.

When Coach Tracker 2 was launched by uTrack, it immediately proved a huge hit with customers accessing it for the very latest real-time accurate information on their coach of choice. The web-based tool enabled users to keep tabs on all 550 coaches any time of the day or night seven days a week.

This cloud-based technology allowed users to download the app for free from the app store and then they could track any service they wish, in real-time as distinct from scheduled time. The customer was confident of where the coach actually was as compared with when it was scheduled to arrive.

In addition, it gave the location of the coach on a map so they could see how near or far it was from their required stop. The clever bit was however, how the system calculates how long it would take for each service to actually arrive at each stop on the journey. That

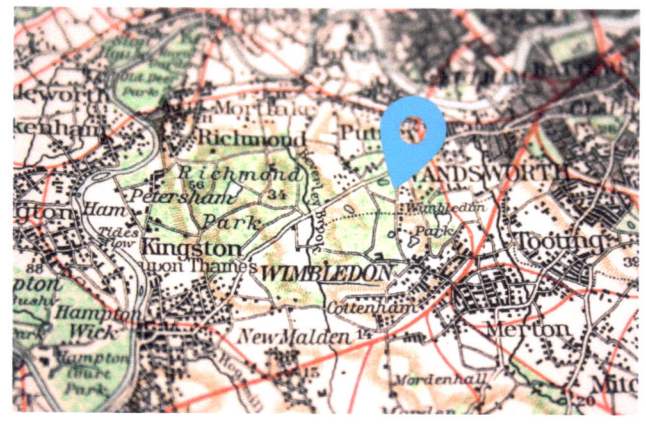

accurate estimate was then displayed every minute. For the first time ever customers standing at stops actually knew when and where their bus would arrive.

Even better if you were waiting for a coach to pick up friends or family and you did not know where the stop was, you could look it up and see what it looked like to enable you to recognise it, and it will tell you when it will arrive. The logic behind that new development was simple - to ensure that it worked over the broadest range of devices; iPhone's, tablets, iPads and Android phones.

Also, the app navigation was enhanced by introducing a sliding menu that appeared on the left-hand side of the screen allowing you to save favourite stops. There was also a broad range of other useful tools such as accessing services and locations. One really clever additional feature was that you could look up your nearest stop, as well as book coach tickets. It was a one-stop-shop solution. for passengers.

The app also gave users the very latest information, care of National Express Twitter feeds, so the very latest updates, offers and news were all at your fingertips.

Coach Tracker had over one and a half million people using it with many making repeat visits through the website. A growing number of thousands downloaded the app.

The breakdown of device usage was also very interesting, with 66% using a mobile device – either a smartphone or a tablet. Further analysis revealed some other very interesting facts. Apple device usage was the highest at 52%, followed very closely by Android at 44% so between them, they clearly dominated the market.

The remaining 4% was provided by the likes of Windows, Blackberry etc, which indicated the huge gap between the two giants and the rest. I would not have thought that it would have been such a huge gap, but we had the facts, quite literally, at our finger tips. However, the really interesting fact that was emerging was that all mobile usage was growing by a staggering 30% every six months. The clear winner, however, was Android usage which was growing twice as fast as iPhone usage.

The icing on the cake for this piece of technology was that uTrack was short-listed in the Innovation category of the highly respected UK Bus Awards and the app was chosen as the 'App of the Week' by the Sun newspaper.

And it didn't stop there!

The adventure continued and for me every day I got to see up close and personal what it looked like in real terms, as I had access to a piece of clever kit that allowed me to see anyone who was using Coach Tracker anywhere in the world. I was addicted to it, one night at midnight there were a total of 13,768 people who had used Coach Tracker mostly in the UK, but there were people looking from all over the world.

There were people from South Korea, France, Czech Republic, Ukraine and Poland all watching individual services. I could see what they were tracking, how long for, what they had tracked before. The business intelligence was huge, and all helped the process of evolving even more clever technology. The most interesting viewing that I saw was from the Imperial Palace of the Emperor of Japan.

It all started with a pint in the Fountain with my dear friend, Alex Perry. That was the first step in a journey of a thousand miles, and it continued - onwards and upwards!

Restructuring...
Moving the Deckchairs

It is quite a common practice that when one takes over a new depot, or indeed company, that one just steps back and watches what goes on. Who does what and who does not do anything.

I have always believed that it is prudent to pause and ponder before acting. The benefits of gradual observation are numerous and varied. It allows you the time to settle in, get around, meet the team and, generally get a feel for how the business is managed.

I recall going to Kidderminster depot on my first day as the grandly titled Divisional Manager Kidderminster and the Wyre Forest. My new empire included a very big, old, rambling, massive depot that included its own ghost.

Today it is now part of a Tesco superstore... not sure what happened to the ghost? It probably got a Saturday job.

It (the depot, not the ghost), employed a fair number of people on services in Kidderminster, Stourport on Severn, and Bewdley as well as an outstation in Bridgenorth.

So, there I was, king of everything that I could see, which, from the knackered old depot, was not really that much if honest. In fairness, the previous manager had been a good guy and had been moved to Digbeth.

I knew the staff quite well as I had covered in the past. It was a steady kind of depot and had some excellent what I call NCOs – men who knew the workforce, the systems and knew their craft. My view was fairly straightforward: if it ain't bust, then don't fix it. All bubbled along quite nicely until the news was broken locally that Brintons, the region's largest carpet manufacturer, was in financial trouble and was going to close down its factories and relocate to a different country. Well, that really put the cat amongst the pigeons!

Within six months, patronage dropped as jobs were lost. Suddenly, Kidderminster found itself with one of the highest rates of unemployment in Europe as the knock-on effect cascaded down. Only one thing for it, we had to cut our cloth accordingly.

So, out went the outstation at Bridgenorth, along with a load of tenders operated under contract to Shropshire County Council. I was given the job of going to County Hall to break the bad news. It went down very badly, as you can understand.

However, that is one of the elements of being a manager, dealing with the good and bad, the easy and the difficult. It was time to rearrange the deck chairs.

So, I had a good old look around and decided that I could strip out three jobs, focusing on shedding the weakest links in the chain. This also meant having to offer retraining amongst those who I wanted to keep. I went through the whole HR process, which is never easy for those on the receiving end although everyone applied for the newly advertised roles.

Following interviews, the new posts were filled and we said adios to those who were not successful. Off we went with fewer people doing more work to support fewer passengers, using fewer buses. And so, welcome to the spiral of decline. I had shuffled the deck chairs on the Titanic for the final time and, in due course, I myself was shuffled – off to Head Office to join the Senior Management Team.

The thing is, that on that rocky road known as the career path, it is necessary to undertake the good and the bad.

As my dear old dad said, and it's true, *'into every life a little rain must fall, so always ensure that your brolly is always close at hand, you will usually find plenty of these lying spare in the lost property office.'*

Well Done NCT's Trojan Horse

The canny team at Nottingham City Transport had a rather good idea they used to a very positive effect with their Trojan Horse idea.

The plan was simple; an apparently normal bus was driven around in areas known to be 'challenging', where incidents of vandalism and anti-social behaviour were higher than average.

The bus, had toughened glass and the bus passengers were plain clothed Police officers, so any disorder could be dealt with swiftly and vigorously. This led to some very real cost savings with reductions of vehicle repair bills dropping from £150,000 right down to an impressive £55,000 over a four year period. Justification in its own right.

A key part of the success was the creation of the Respect for Transport Campaign, run in conjunction with the Police and Community Protection teams. It illustrated that the best solutions stem from good partnerships and working together.

A similar process was used in the West Midlands, with a bespoke Police team working with Centro to target problem areas. The team was led by an Inspector and they gathered intelligence where vandalism occurred and ran specific campaigns. They made a significant impact and helped improve the image of the bus as a safe experience.

When I worked for the Diamond Bus Company in Birmingham we operated the Nifty 50, as we called it, in competition with National Express West Midlands. Locally, it was nicknamed the Cannabis Express, not the most endearing image, with tales of OAPs innocently popping into town and finding themselves stoned and unable to get off. It invoked images of bad 1970s zombie films.

I atteneded some passenger focus group meetings in Maypole where the service terminated. Listening to the unpleasant experiences it was a wonder anyone ever bothered attempting to get on the bus.

The truth though was very different. The majority had a perfectly acceptable experience without any real drama. The other thing that I found was that drivers who experienced regular problems did so because they didn't always have the right skills to deal with potential problems.

I recall when I was at Hereford I joined a gym called The Factory. It was run by an ex-SAS trooper called 'Come back Ginger'. Apparently the nickname 'Come back' was given for his exploits in Afghanistan when he helped the Mujahidin fight the Russian

special forces, the legendary 'Spetnaz'. The other lads in the regiment didn't expect him to return from what were suicide missions, but miraculously he did and then retired. He was extremely fit and a good bloke. As I got to know him we discussed self-defence training for drivers and he kindly offered, for a nominal fee, to hold a self-defence course for the bus drivers. I ran it past the lads and they thought it would be a great idea.

So, one sunny Sunday afternoon, 40 of us pitched up at the gym where Ginger showed us his skills, mostly on me, which was greatly appreciated by the drivers.

Three hours later, we were off to the pub to lick our wounds. All was fine and dandy until the next day when I had a phone call from the editor of The Hereford Times asking if it was true that the SAS had been drafted in to teach self-defence to the drivers of Hereford Depot.

Oh God, I thought.

"How did you find this out?" I asked.

"Easily, we had an anonymous call from one of your drivers claiming that being a bus driver was such a dangerous job that the infamous SAS had been called in."

Well, blood drained from the face and a nasty feeling landed in the stomach. What to do? I told the editor that I needed to take advice and I rang big Ken, the MD.

"Oh my God, we will never recruit another bus driver again, do you know who told him?"

"No, I have not got a clue."

Unbeknownst to me, the Hereford Times had already sent a photographer down to the canteen to snap the bus drivers in various pugilistic poses.

One of said drivers had donned a balaclava just to add some authenticity.

The genie was out of the bottle and it was headline news. It went national and was covered across the nation.

I received mixed reviews; some thought it was great publicity, others thought it gave a negative image of the job, but all it was really was a bit of advice back in the days before NCT's Trojan Horse.

Pile Drivers

Back in the good old days when I did my PCV driving test, the world seemed a much more relaxed place. Not sure if that is fair or not, but maybe as you get older your perspective alters. *'Nostalgia ain't what it used to be,'* someone once said.

My salad days memories are surprisingly lucid, given that I can seldom remember my own name these days.

My bus driver training was very simple. I would catch the number 36 bus at 07:30 from outside my flat in the small village of Killinghall, in Harrogate, and then present myself to the driver training school where my good friend, Mr Arnold Lofthouse, the senior driving instructor and examiner, would despatch me and two other lads with Pete, the most experienced instructor.

There we would attend the canteen for an obligatory brew and then be led to mount our mighty steed. In this case, it was a converted London Route Master bus which had been adapted for dual control.

We would then take it in turns to drive this lovely old bus around the truly outstanding Yorkshire countryside, gorgeous places like Hebden Bridge, a really lovely way to spend your days. Gradually, day in, day out, we started to master the skills needed to be a good driver. I look back with fondness on those happy and fulfilling days.

The bus had a personality all of its own, it needed to be treated with respect, if you did not then it would let you know. The reason being that to drive it you had to double de-clutch it. This meant taking it out of gear, then getting the revs right to put it into the next required gear. Failure to get this complex manoeuvre right would result in a severe whack to the shin by said pedal, I certainly received my fair share in the early days, but over time you got to know the bus, and the bus got to know you.

So, eventually, I passed my test and all was fine and dandy. In truth I never really did a lot of bus driving, I liked meeting the people and all that, but shifts take some getting used to in fairness. But it is all part of it, and I personally took the view that said if you are going to manage bus drivers then you need to understand what it is like to drive a bus.

The sands of time passed by and suddenly at the age of 45, I receive a letter telling me that I have to go to the company doctor for a medical. I duly reported to the doctor's surgery located next to the depot in Padmore Street in Worcester one hot Friday afternoon.

The deal was simple, every month end

Friday was bus driver medical day and as I walked in, I was surrounded by a collection of what appeared to be members of a rugby union team, all dressed as bus drivers. Big, burly men with large bulky girths and tight-fitting uniforms, most of whom seemed to be sporting brightly coloured tattoos.

Silence descended as I entered because some recognised me as being a member of management, and most of them had sat opposite me at disciplinary interviews... all a bit awkward; mostly for me.

I took a seat and spoke to the very large man sitting next to me. His name was Smurf – I had no idea what his real name was, indeed he may not have had one but apparently, he looked like Papa Abraham from the Smurfs. I thought that it was because he looked a bit purple.

Anyway, polite conversation ensued, as I asked him how he was. Big mistake, he then proceeded to give me a very detailed anatomical explanation as to the debilitating effect of his piles, or haemorrhoids. Frankly, I was nearly sick on the spot.

"The thing is," he said, "the Mrs said that they are the size of grapes."

Dear Mother of God I thought, surely she has not had to view said offensive articles?

Now in full flow and attracting a small audience of equally horrified eavesdroppers, he continued, "Yes, each night she has to apply this gel."

At which point he produced it from his pocket. For one horrifying moment I thought that he was going to invite me to have a go.

"The trouble is she works nights, so then I have to get my oldest kid to do it."

Oh, Dear Lord, surely a job for social services I was thinking.

"So how old is your daughter?" I asked. "She is 21 and a nurse, so she knows exactly what she is doing. In fact, it's brought us closer together."

Utter silence now.

"Yes I imagine that it would. I honestly don't think that you could get closer than that." I stuttered, now truly traumatized.

I don't remember the medical. As I wandered into the doctor's surgery he turned and looked at me and said, "Oh, you don't look very well, you have gone very white... have a seat."

"Oh, no thanks, I would prefer to stand."

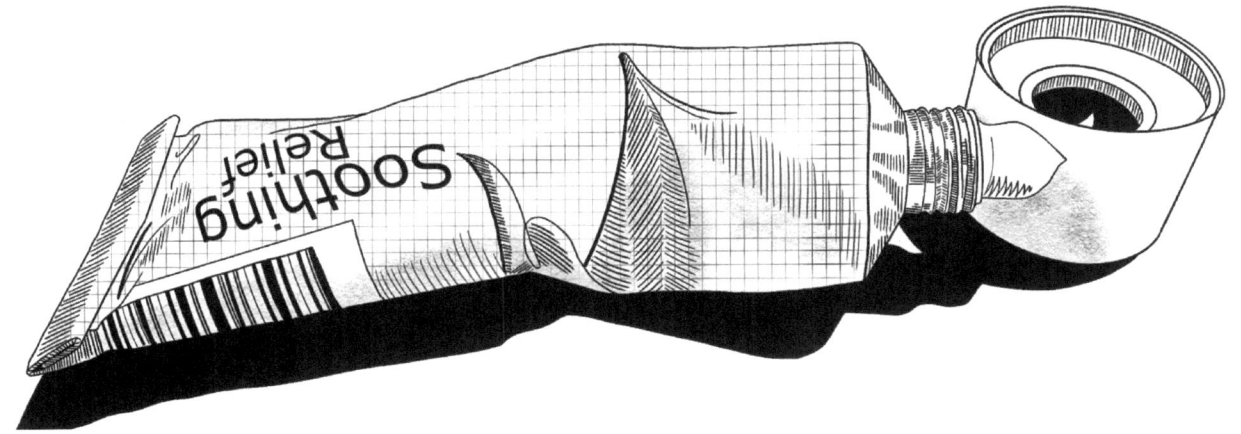

Roadtrip...

Well, after nearly two years the key team from uTrack finally organised a road trip and we all flew to Warsaw, Poland for a lad's weekend of relaxing socialising and sightseeing. For me personally, it was also a clashing of two of my worlds, as the world of uTrack met with Verita HR, the Polish company of which I was the Managing Director.

What a great time we had, the hotel that we stayed at was the excellent InterContinental Hotel, one of the tallest buildings in Warsaw and located virtually next door to the iconic Palace of Culture, the monument to Soviet domination that was gifted by the Russian communists to the good people of Poland. And so, with a classic sense of irony, the Poles nicknamed the Palace 'The birthday cake' because that was what it looks like.

The InterContinental's excellent gym and pool is on the 39th floor, it is the highest gym in Western Europe and has massive glass windows, so the views as you sweat are panoramic; truly a great experience that I took advantage of every day that I was there.

The idea was to just spend time together as a team and that is what we did. I took the lads to meet the team at Verita, with their really smart, professional office located in the heart of Warsaw's business district. We also did some work and met with Warsaw's biggest tram company, ZTM.

We also arranged to meet for a meal in a lovely traditional Polish restaurant located in the heart of the Old Town, lovingly restored after 85 per cent of the city was levelled by the

Nazis. And then afterwards off to a nightclub to bop the night away, happy days indeed.

The following day we embarked on a three-hour Segway tour of Warsaw. The first five minutes of straddling a Segway is a bit like getting on a horse, if honest I was a tad Bambi-like as I got used to it, but after five minutes we were all gallivanting like race horses.

It really was an excellent way to see a city and you cover a lot of ground as these machines can reach speeds of 18 kilometres an hour. We were also fortunate to have an excellent guide. Olga was super enthusiastic and very clued up as we learned about Warsaw's history, palaces, invasions and dominations.

The story of Warsaw is not complete without the tragedy of war: the heroic Siege of Warsaw, the utter destruction of the Jewish community and the wholesale deportation to the death camps is vividly brought home when you see the memorials peppered around the city.

However, be under no illusion, while it is imperative to rightly remember the past, today Warsaw is right at the heart of new Europe. Its economy is vibrant and the city has a sense of optimism and growth. I feel it more every time I go, which is about six times a year.

We had a great time and we are already planning our next trip which will be to a very different country, but that's the point of these adventures. It is to live life to the full and enjoy the benefits of a shared vision and we are starting to live the dream.

Utrack
Ten Years on

In a galaxy far, far, away there was once a group of five young Jedis, (well four young ones and one older Yoda type, ie me) who shared a dream and a vision. The dream was to change bus and coach travel in a positive way by using technology. The vision was to create a strong and vibrant company. Interestingly, almost ten years on from joining the uTrack family, it was amazing to take a little bit of time to stop, reflect, and ponder; one of my favourite phrases, given to me by my dear old dad. To reflect on what has been achieved from humble beginnings to where we were ten years on.

So, late one Thursday night I decided to look back. The first pitch that I was ever involved with was with the legend that is Scott Dunn. Scott,

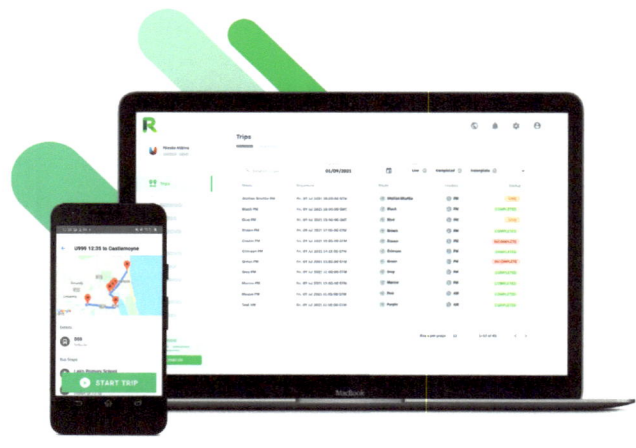

back in 2008, was the gifted buccaneering MD of the Diamond Bus Company where I was employed as the Commercial Manager. Scott kindly agreed to let uTrack monitor four bespoke vehicles operating on a route from Redditch to Birmingham, the Worcestershire County Council subsidised 192. What I saw for the first time in my bus career allowed me to actually see minute-by-minute exactly what these buses and, even more importantly, just what the drivers were doing.

It's hard to imagine that in those days, once a bus left the depot basically that was it, you had no idea where it was and what it was doing. Nowadays, young managers take this monitoring and technology for granted and rightly so. For me, however, this was a Damascus moment and it had a profound effect on me, I felt that this clever witchcraft built by Eamonn and Conor was the future of the Bus and Coach Industry. Long story short, I left Diamond and joined the team. Back then it was the three of us along with the gifted artistic genius that was Carlos Anazco, who left his native Venezuela and sought his fortune in Ireland and a brilliant techie, the amazing Valdas from Lithuania. Table for five, please.

Our first break came care of Alex Perry, then the Operations Director for National Express Coach Company. The very day after I left Diamond, July 9th 2009, Alex and I met in a pub in my village called the Fountain and I told him all about uTrack. He was interested and that was the start. As they say, from little acorns mighty oak trees grow. Alex agreed to a trial on a particularly challenging route from Liverpool to Manchester and Leeds, serving the airports. Such was its unreliability that each month thousands would be spent on taxis after passengers complained the coach was late or early, or never turned up. As flights were involved, they could not afford to take chances. Post the trial, any complaints could be investigated immediately at the touch of a historic replay button, and a map in real-time sent to the person complaining. Overnight the complaints stopped, as some people realised the gravy train was no longer available.

And that was just the start, Alex had vision and patience, as he realised just how profound this technology was. Now, ten years on, we are engaged with National Express Coach having enjoyed ten years as a supplier and partner. uTrack worked with First UK Bus, Greyhound Coach across the vast continent of North America, along with First Student who carried over six and a half million students across the USA every school day. Go Ahead Dublin and Hinckley Point power station, were also customers. And more were getting on board all the time.

Ten years on and there were a few more than the Famous Five and a celebration for that auspicious anniversary was held; a super family fun day at a lovely castle just outside Dublin. There were some 50 plus people who attended: employees, partners and their children. It was a great success and the team played, ate, drank and laughed together.

It is great to consider what happened on that journey and it was a source of pride that it managed to have an impact on an industry that has always been very close to my life and times. I was born into the Bus Industry, my dad was formally the General Manager of National Express, so for me working with National Express whilst with uTrack was a natural fit, it completed the circle if you like.

Beauty is in the Eye of the Beholder

Is it possible to view a bus and find it attractive, or indeed ugly? Well, frankly, yes is the simple answer, and how do you create an attractive bus design? Is it an aesthetic question or a simple 'I like that colour, it will do?'

When I was at Diamond Bus, we decided that we wanted to create a unique identity that combined memories of the Midland Red Bus Company in Worcestershire with a modern, new, fresh, 21st-century flair. We also desired something bright, innovative and head-turning for the Black Diamond brand to operate in and around the Black Country.

We went to Ray Stenning, who created an iconic brand both for his buses and himself – a true individualist who lived by his principles. I first met Ray when he attended a meeting at Worcestershire County Council. His style and flamboyance, especially set against the leafy conservative drab predictability of the elderly lady Tory councillors, was a joy to watch. Quite frankly, they never stood a chance.

I was a big fan from that moment on and watched and admired the significant and influential impact that Ray and his team have had around the country ever since. I also believe that his whole ethos towards design and perception have done a lot to subconsciously elevate the public's image of the bus and its status in society.

Imagine being sat behind an old, knackered, Leyland National. Dirty, bits hanging off and fumes gushing out from a ropy exhaust, etc., then compare it to being sat behind a bright, clean, Go Ahead Oxford gleaming, modern

bus, in a fresh red livery with a clever, witty image and caption extolling the virtues of clean air (again, one of Ray's finest).

It's not hard to understand how one will think about the bus set against such dramatic contrasts – the Industry by nature, in my experience, is conservative. I believe that we need the Ray Stennings, and others with his flair and vision, to elevate our stature, and what I say is 'more power to your elbow, Mr Stenning'.

Lifestyle Changes
What Impact on the Bus Industry?

I do not know about you, but would you describe yourself as a creature of habit? What I mean by that is, do you tend to do the same things, in the same way, on a regular basis? Take something very basic like shopping – you know that most basic of requirements. Do you like to do the weekly shop at the same place, paying attention to the latest bargains? Or do you just pop out on a daily basis and get what you fancy when you need it? Of course, a lot depends on your options. If, for example, you own a car, it is of course much easier than if you do not, when you are restricted by what you can carry, compared to what you can load into the car and take home with you.

When I was the manager of Hereford Depot I did a deal with a chap who was the manager of a very large Tesco store in the heart of the city centre. Basically, what I did was transfer all the routes that used multiple terminal points around the city that created all sorts of issues and complications and plonked the whole lot into Tesco's.

Overnight, this resulted in two things, one predictable and one not. The obvious was the immediate improvement in punctuality and reliability which, before we transferred the operation, we were not exactly certain it was going to pay off. But it all worked out for the best, thank the Lord. Had it failed, then not to put too fine a point on it, my job may well have been the price that I would have to pay. But, I always thought that it would work, and we made damn sure that it did.

The other rather interesting consequence, that I had not considered, was the knock-on effect of extra shoppers for Tesco. What actually happened was that because people were suddenly waiting for a bus in a bus station that was basically part of the Tesco superstore, the passengers became shoppers.

After six months, the store had become the UK's biggest, what in retail they call, single basket shopping, whereby the good folk of Hereford would pop in and pick up what they needed on their way home. So, it was a win-win, nearly all round.

Ironically, those who lost out were the shops that used to be located next to the old terminal stops. I was widely abused by the newsagents who overnight watched a plummet in their profits as the schoolkids and pensioners who used to pop in transferred their loyalty and cash into Tesco's.

So, how does today's modern world impact on the life and times of the UK Bus Industry? Well, the truth is that technology and lifestyles have changed dramatically. Today's online shopping world means that your weekly shop can be done for you and delivered direct to your kitchen. No need to go on the bus anymore.

In addition, today's youngsters, and indeed not so young people, do not tend to go to the cinema or indeed the pub as I used to do once upon a time. They are more than happy to stay at home and play Call Of Duty or whatever it is called this week. This allows for complete strangers around the world to stay up all night killing make-believe, virtual other people till the early hours of the morning, rendering them useless for anything else for the remainder of the day.

This has a knock-on effect as it means people do not go out on the bus to meet other people as I used to do. Not only that but it also means that as they have options to work from home as I now do now, they do not go to work at the office or factory. That means that transport habits have changed and not necessarily for the better from the Bus Industry's point of view.

What this means is, that the Bus Industry has to be agile and nimble, but that is the nature of today's modern world, where your phone will be your ticket, your journey planner, and your bank account.

I am not sure what the single basket shopper from Hereford would have made of it all.

There it is, life in the modern world.

Monster School Bus

That bastion of public transport, Mr Phil Tonks, once posted a most amusing video on Facebook that any lover of the good old bus would enjoy watching. Basically it was an average American school bus that has been converted into a monster truck.

It was seen in all its glory, majestically meandering across the course, squashing large numbers of big American cars and defying gravity as it crashed and leapt its way around. Much to the joy of the hordes of monster truck/bus fans lining the course.

This got me thinking about the other iconic images of the good old American school bus, perhaps the most famous being the bus driver from the Simpsons, Otto Mann. The headphone-wearing, cool, guitar playing, somewhat bad bus driver for Springfield Elementary School, his driving record speaks for itself. Fifteen accidents and not a single fatality, and as for his motto in life, *My name is Otto and I love to get Blotto,* that may well explain the volume of accidents.

I found myself in a spot of bother with my daughter a while ago as I was commenting on the various disciplinary infringements that Otto was indulging in, when I was told quite forcibly to leave the office in the office and just watch the Simpsons! Fair comment.

This also reminded me of when I was a student studying, amongst other things, English Literature. My tutor was a lovely man, an ex-Oxford chap who had a real and natural gift for literature and poetry. Our little group of students had been joined by a new boy, well, actually, he was a former Police detective

in his 40s who had decided, rather bravely, to change careers and wanted to become a teacher.

So, this chap joins the group who were all trying to understand Macbeth and, frankly, he struggled. His previous training had made his approach very rigid. He was starting to get despondent when the tutor took him to one side and suggested that he studied Macbeth in terms of a crime scene, and to catalogue the varied offences that the Bard had created. Well, that was it! He was in his element. Suddenly, this guy was on fire, he played to all his strengths and his previous experience. And that, of course, is the mark of a great teacher: someone who can bring out the potential that they see in others.

So, back to the real issue. Do we in the UK think that the USA school bus model could ever work in the UK? I know that First and others have looked at it in the past and various local authorities have experimented. Indeed, some businesses have created their own niche market (Green Bus Company in Birmingham is a good example), but as a national agenda, I think that such a window for it to ever exist has gone.

Warsaw or Walsall?

I don't know if, as I get older, that my powers of speech appear to be failing me or I am just mumbling more than I used to. It was brought home to me in the steam room at my local gym.

I had done my usual daily routine and been for my swim and then popped into the steam room for a spot of reflection and soul-searching. I have been going to the gym for decades and there is, I notice, a certain protocol that is followed by virtually everyone.

The funny thing is that no one ever openly talks about it, but the rules of engagement are quite simple:

Never make eye contact directly.

Never openly stare at attractive members of the opposite sex.

Never, under any circumstances, attempt to engage in conversation, as this immediately gets clocked by everyone else who is doing exactly the same as you.

Great mirth can be had when watching other hapless souls attempt to engage in conversation with people they are blatantly attempting to hit upon. As for me, I like to be anonymous to the point of invisible. However, there is a certain degree of potential conversation that can be had in certain safe, or what I like to call neutral, zones.

Zone one is the swimming pool, where again it is good form to allow the person in front of you to go first, as it were. If you happen to be quicker than the person before you then good form should usually elicit a quick, "No, no after you, you are quicker than me."

I have often been tempted to reply with a quick, "Well frankly you big fat porker, I certainly am." But being a gentleman I could never bring myself to be so harsh, or as they like to call it in Poland, honest.

So there I am, minding my own business in the semi gloom that is the steam room.

Inside there is another person, a lady, as ever I assume my place which again protocol dictates is to sit as far away as possible and look straight ahead to avoid the shame of being labelled a starer.

Anyway, out of the blue and without any provocation the shadowy figure speaks, "How far did you swim?"

"Ten lengths," I reply quick as lighting.

"Oh, I have seen you here a few times," she said.

Oops thinks I, this is a tad unfamiliar for me.

"Well I try to attend on a regular basis, but I was away last weekend."

"Oh really?" says the lady, "Where were you?"

"I was in Warsaw, in Poland."

"Oh really," she replied, "Noddy Holder is from there is he not?"

Alarm bells now ringing loudly, Noddy Holder from Warsaw? Now I am a big Slade fan and had the privilege of meeting the great man at a wedding a few years ago, but one thing I do know, he certainly never came from Poland.

Getting slightly awkward now – what to do? Agree or point out that Noddy was not from Poland.

"Err, well, possibly," I reply.

To which came the immortal line...

"Just that you might have bumped into him when you said that you were in Walsall at Iceland."

Proper diction and speak from the stomach is what my old drama teacher used to teach, now he would be spinning in his grave.

The Wonderful Little Red Book

One of my titles during my career was *Chairman of the Bus and Coach Forum of the Chartered Institute of Logistics and Transport*. Now I don't know why, but whenever I write that I am reminded of the classic scene in Gladiator, when Russell Crowe gives his impassioned speech explaining that he is not an ordinary gladiator, but in fact Maximus Aurelius, father to a murdered son, Commander of the northern legions, etc.

Point is, his title is a tad longer than that above.

Anyway, I digress. The point that I am going to make is this: tucked away on an industrial estate, in Corby, was the Head Office of the Institute. And therein lies what

Photo by Viv Ainslie from her own collection of CDs.

I choose to call, arguably the UK's best-kept secret. It comes in two parts, the first is the Knowledge and Learning Centre, which is a wonderful purpose-built library, housing a hoard of treasures that are all accessible to members. Should you have required any help, any information, or a host of other extremely worthwhile data, then all you had to do was email, ring or arrange to pop in.

The second gem was the guru who sat behind this, the charming and enthusiastic Mr Peter Huggins, who, with his small, but willing, team, ran the whole shooting match. Now, if Peter had not been a librarian and archivist, I believe that he could have been an announcer for Radio 4, possibly the shipping reports. He had one of those voices that resonates calmness and knowledge, and gave the visitor the sense that if there was one place in the world where you could find information, then that was the place. Verbal hugs you might say - he was well-named

And so it came to pass that I decided we would attempt an audit on the members of the Bus and Coach Forum.

Who actually are the people who run these Companies? And what sort of snapshot could we take to get a proper feel for the people in the Forum and in the business? So, a couple of trips and a bit of research later, we came up with a simple, but cunning, plan that we hoped would engage our present members.

So, 251 members were sent an email, from my good self as the Chairman of the Court of King Caractacus.

In the email I asked the following very simple questions:

- who are you and what do you do? (fairly simple so far)
- how many vehicles do you have
- how many staff
- how many routes do you operate?

My thinking was simple; if I was sent this, I would do one of two things, either I would reply immediately, or I would come back to it later... or not do it all. Yes OK that was three!

Lessons learned: timing is always important. August is holiday month so don't bother, wait until mid-September when the schools are back, and normal routine has returned. The second thing, is maybe make the tone slightly less formal, suffice to say that there are more ways to skin the proverbial cat, or is that rabbit?

Plan B was as a result of a very nice present Peter gave me. It was called The Little Red Book 2012 - not to be confused with a little black book that I owned back in my youth... happy days.

No, sadly – and this I blame on the ageing process – the truth was that I derived as much pleasure from the little red book as I once did from the little black book back in the day. Suffice to say, it was an absolute goldmine which included everything and everyone. It truly was the ultimate transport directory. It covered a full trade directory, Tendering and Regulatory Authorities, Organisations and Societies, British Isle Operators, and Tram and Bus Rapid Transit Systems. It was a real labour of love and I imagine that was the sort of task that is like painting the Forth Bridge - you get it completed only to start all over again. It depended on all participants keeping them up to date. So, my friends, thanks to the kindness of Peter, I found Bus and Coach Damascus.

One final thing – if I had taken out all the people who replied to the audit for a meal, as it stood, I think that a McDonald's Happy Meal would probably have sufficed, but I am not finished.

As my dear old dad used to say, "Hope beats eternal in the human breast."

Onwards and Upwards.

Take a Gander at Uganda

The President's lunch for the Chartered Institute of Logistics and Transport took place recently in Central London. This prestigious bash saw the baton being handed over from Graham Inglis to Jim Steer.

I had to say well done to Graham, he did a very good job following the excellent year in office of Sir Peter Hendy, from TfL, whose tenure preceded his. As I was involved in the Safety Forum set up by Darren Bradley, also from DHL, I got to see and understand how the freight and logistics world operated. And, in truth, I was very impressed, it was very slick and professional with some really able and capable people.

The Safety Forum was a real success, and that was driven by Graham and implemented by Darren and a small, but dedicated, team. Of course, Graham did a huge amount in that year and when I heard Jim Steer give his inaugural speech about his expectations and

intentions, it was clear that the ship was yet again in very safe hands. So, it was well done Graham, and good luck Jim.

So where does Uganda fit in, I hear you ask?

Well, over lunch I sat next to a very affable young man called Gary Forster, who was the Chief Executive of Transaid, the charity jointly set up by CILT. It was fascinating to listen to Gary's journey within the world of delivering positive and lifesaving projects across the world, but mostly in Africa.

At one point his phone rang and he said he had to pop out for a moment. When he came back he said that there was a bit of a problem as the President of Nigeria had just decreed that a part of the country had just been declared a no-go zone as Al Qaida rebels had infiltrated it. As Gary had people about to enter that neck of the woods, it was prudent to rethink tactics. Talk about crisis management! That puts a bit of lost mileage, or a dip in revenue, in perspective,

Meanwhile, back in Uganda. I think that it might have been Private Eye who many years ago invented the very funny euphemism that any politicians engaging in illicit sexual malarkey would henceforth be seen to be indulging in 'Ugandan Relations'.

I can happily say that the only activity that took place in 2013 was of the fund-raising variety, in the form of The Uganda Cycle Challenge. That life-changing experience took place from 2-10 November of that year and the challenge was to see if you had what it took to cycle over 430 kilometres, in five days, across the wetlands and fruit plantations of stunning Uganda.

Catching Buses in Germany

Whilst I love the Bus Industry I am most certainly not a bus spotter. I can, from an aesthetic point of view, appreciate a good design and livery - I especially enjoy a classic Ray Stenning art work.

But the very prospect of spending time with a notebook taking down numbers and taking photos has never appealed to me personally, but fair play to those happy souls who do enjoy such activities and the best of luck to them as well.

What I do enjoy, and my dear old chum Roger French will resonate with this, is the experience of using bus services and enjoying the views and the people. The joy is even better when done in a foreign country. So it was that I managed to survive the experience

of catching two trains from Dusseldorf to Paderborn, without obvious stress, the day before and next day it was time to catch the bus.

It was also a bit of a laugh to travel on German buses in the company of the good Doctor. My first impression was that the fleets that I saw were clean, generally modern, and actually a bit more expensive than I anticipated. We strolled out of her parents' house to the bus stop, which had easy to read timetables, but no obvious electronic displays. Interestingly, the house is located next door to a truly huge British Army barracks, so around the bus stop itself were English notices for hand car washes, and well known British brands were advertised in shops, which was a tad disorienting.

So, as you boarded the bus there was a control process which means that you had to pay the driver and then he released a pass bar that you pushed past. We got two singles at €2.50 each and I noted they did not offer returns, which I thought was interesting. The bus was articulated and the seats that we had were clean and presentable, as was the floor of the bus, with no sign of litter.

There were audio announcements, all in German although a third of those on the bus were Brits. There were quite a lot of direct marketing announcements all promoting discounted tickets. No delightful anti-social UK announcements that we 'enjoy' on some of our UK buses asking people if they had blood in their poo, or any sexually transmitted diseases.

Other observations were that if you were due to catch a connecting bus and the service was operating late, the driver would communicate that to the required driver who would wait for you. I had certainly not come across that in the UK and the good Doctor advised me that she used to regularly take advantage of the facility. Also of interest was the fact that after a certain time, I think 18:30, you could ask the driver to let you off in between stops and they would do so. Now imagine that in the UK, a license for bedlam over here as we expect a door-to-door service do we not!

So, overall a positive experience, the drivers displayed that professional aloofness that only bus drivers can produce, but when I tried to buy two tickets in German he played the game and when I replied *'Danke'*, he replied and smiled. Mind you we are all the same, if you make the effort then in my experience 99.9 per cent do likewise.

So it was a good experience, in my view, efficient, ordered, clean and punctual and so I will give German buses 7.5 out 10.

Das ist gut Jah!

Utrack Help the Hunters

So, there I was sat minding my own business watching the telly on a busy Monday night, after a long day at work and then a bit of hard graft at the gym, when a new TV show appeared before my eyes on Channel 4, called Hunted. Now this has been on before, but to be honest I had never seen it and it looked quite interesting. The principle was simple enough and goes right back to the very beginning of time itself, where Neolithic man used to hunt, well, other Neolithic men. Thinking back to childhood, some of the earliest games that you ever play involve hunting each other. *Hide and Seek* is a good example; who can forget the thrill of spotting a friend hidden away behind a tree or under a bed or, when you get older, finding someone you do not know under your ex-wife's bed, but that is another game.

So the situation was clear; ten ordinary members of the public were selected by the programme makers to be dumped in a particular location. They then had to use their wits, guile, and ingenuity to avoid a group of very well-trained former Police and military detectives and investigators, and basically not get caught.

The show started with a brief introduction of the key hunters. Led by a grizzled ex-Scotland Yard detective of the Reagan and Carter Sweeney Todd mould Sweeney Todd is cockney rhyming slang for the Flying Squad, the once infamous anti-robbery squad that was a key part of the Metropolitan Police. They were notoriously hard, and close encounters with the villains would often result in the bad guys having to have a Richard The Third, to quote another well-known Cockney slang expression.

This hard-nosed 'seen it all before' cop was joined by a very smooth former sniper, who was also an expert in concealment. They were supported by a big team in the control centre, and a collection of out-on-the-road teams who drove Range Rovers, and an 'eye in the sky' surveillance helicopter, backed

up by a small army of high performance drones; very useful when searching for people in rural areas. To be honest, given the pedigree of the hunters, I was mildly surprised that there was anybody left after the first ten minutes. Interestingly, the hunted were a strange collection: a deputy mayor; a father and son team; a retired head teacher, and a former police officer.

The programme followed the hunted being driven into inner City Manchester where they all promptly legged it, seemingly without any real plan to escape capture other than to run to ground and hide amongst the masses. The former mayor of Bradford legged it straight into a Subway fast-food outlet, where he persuaded a man shaped nothing like him to don his blue coat and pretend to be him. Genius you might think until the guy just strolled out into the street like he was taking a walk in the park. Even I, the untrained bloke on the couch, could see that this clearly was not the mayor, who then scarpered at full pelt whilst swearing like a trooper.

However, what really stole the show for me was when a nice elderly lady, who I believe was once a head teacher, decided that the best way to escape was to pop to Chorlton Street Coach Station and catch a nice National Express Coach down to Milton Keynes. One small snag, however, was the fact that the hunters were able to scrutinise CCTV footage to identify her ticket and destination. Low and behold, the show tracked her getting on the coach, chatting to passengers, it even had a nice shot of the Coach Tracker logo for good measure. The hunters were licking their lips as they followed her progress down south and the team were ready and waiting to pounce at Milton Keynes.

And then she threw a clever curved ball, as they approached Milton Keynes she asked the driver if he had anyone to pick up, he said no, then she asked the passengers if anyone wanted to get off, again a resounding no.

So, the Hunters could only watch with dismay as the coach thundered past Milton Keynes on its way to London. However despite her best efforts to camouflage herself by wearing a different hat, good old Coach Tracker could still track the journey and, sadly, as soon as she got off they nabbed her.

Game over, all part of the service.

Coach Tracker and Hunters: 1

Hunted old lady: 0.

Sweet F.A.

I recall talking to one of the UK bus world's biggest characters – none other than Mr Roger Davies, a renowned author, as well as a man who ran a very tidy bus company in Maidstone and District. Roger led the management buyout when all of the National bus companies were tasked with being sold off, and like a few fortunate people, he did a good job and, eventually, sold the business and set sail into the sunset.

However, you cannot keep a good man down and Roger was one of the most passionate transport professionals that I have encountered – always happy to travel the length and breadth of the UK and beyond. He presented extensively and was a most amusing raconteur with a library of anecdotes of his life and times on the buses.

So, there we were, Roger enjoying a most convivial white wine and me manfully downing my fresh orange juice, when he tells me about a chap who worked as a cleaner at a bus depot in Cumbria. This chap worked the same shift, so unlike anyone else, he was on a permanent line as they called it. This particular gent was called Francis Albert Sweet and he had been there for some 30 years and was dearly loved by all.

Therefore, it was decided that he should be suitably rewarded with his own special line at the very top of the duties, therefore, whenever anybody wished to go and look at the rota, they were greeted with the immortal line:

Duties for Today...

Sweet F.A.

Lovely, and fairly typical of the humour that one often encounters up and down bus depots across the land.

Never Underestimate the Power of the Tap

I think it is only human to want to feel as though we belong to something, it might be country, a religion, a sect, a football team, (to some the last three are in fact the same). It is almost a primeval part of that awkwardness that we all feel when we walk into an event, or a school, or an office, or a pub, or maybe even a club, where we don't know anyone, and you just want to quietly float in and merge into the background. What you most definitely do not want to do is to embarrass yourself or in some way end up feeling awkward.

And what exactly has that got to do with anything I hear you ask? Well, let me enlighten you?

Picture the scene. My dad, John Austin Birks, in 1983 was the General Manager of the mighty Midland Red Bus Company. It was a massive company employing tens of thousands of people across a large chunk of Middle England and beyond. He was also the Chairman of the West Midlands section of the then Chartered Institute of Transport. I was a young aspiring Senior Management Trainee having just started what was to be my three-year apprenticeship with the National Bus Company. Dad had suggested that it would be a good idea if I joined him at a local event that was happening at a very swanky venue in Birmingham, so I happily agreed to go with him.

Not ever being a drinker, he was more than happy to drive us to the venue, which was already packed by the time that we arrived. Being the grand fromage, on arrival he was busy meeting and greeting, leaving me pretty much to my own devices. I did not know a single person in the venue, why would I? So I did what I usually do in such circumstances, I meander around and work out the lay of the land. The first job was to find some liquid refreshment, and it does not take me long to hone in on the young lady handing out large goblets of red wine. I discreetly necked a couple quite swiftly, realising that the freebies were limited and once the formalities kicked off out went the free booze. I was feeling much more relaxed as I liberated glass number three. At that point the five-minute warning was given, so I thought it best to neck it asap, pop to the loo and then position myself at the back and observe. Like those who circulate within spy circles, I simply wanted to be the classic grey man.

So, off I went and did what I had to do, and I then thought as ever it best to wash my hands. And this is where the trouble started.

The hotel had these taps that you pushed the nozzle down and out came the H2O. What I had not anticipated was the speed, volume, and power that the water would have.

Honestly it was like a tsunami. Seriously, it splashed everywhere, all over my face and hair, my jacket, but even worse, all across the top of my trousers. It was a calamity of the highest possible magnitude. To all intents and purposes it seemed as though I had suffered a hugely humiliating accident. Crestfallen I had a moment of panic, what could I do? Only one thing for it, the hand dryers were my only salvation, but tragically their trajectory was

too high for my trouser line. So, while I could dry my face jacket and upper torso, below stairs it was a shipping forecast nightmare.

By now I could hear the crowd taking their positions, I did my best to limit the damage, but thought best option, discreetly slide out, get a chair at the back and let nature take its course and dry said affected clothing as best possible. So, after counting to ten out I went, and straight into the horrendous glare of public spotlight, I could not have timed it worse.

I thought that I had slid to the back of the auditorium, and would be sat at the back. Unbeknown to me, all that I had managed to do was walk out of the loo, that was actually parallel to the podium where my dad was stood.

Indeed, as I realised the enormity of my error, he actually said, as he copped me from the corner of his eye, "And here is my son, Austin, who has joined me for his first ever CIT meeting."

Luckily he did not seem to notice the fact that it looked like my excitement at attending my first ever CIT meeting had resulted in a momentary lack of control of my waterworks, accentuated quite gloriously by my light grey suit.

Obviously the capacity crowd had clocked the wardrobe malfunction immediately. I recall the faint barrage of collective giggling break out, although to be fair they were very kind. I grabbed the first, quite soon to be soggy, seat that I could find and sat the event out. My dad, God bless him, never said a single word.

To this day, I don't know if he'd realised the exact nature of my misfortune. Or, more likely being the kind man that he was he chose not to embarrass me knowing that I had already done that to myself quite nicely thank you.

The Simple Joy of a Bus Ride

Can you remember the very first time that you went on a bus? I don't mean one of those children's carousel rides, where they would invariably include a fun double-decker bus, I mean a real one, where the best seat in the house was naturally upstairs on the front seats, preferably on the right above where the driver sits. It was only right that you sat there and pretended to be the bus driver. Happy childhood days indeed. It also begs the question at what age do you stop wanting to be that uninhibited child? Answers on a postcard.

From being the happy, young child pretending to be the driver, before I knew it I was the bus driver. At the tender age of 23 there I was sat in the cab of a former Routemaster London bus, driving around the unadulterated beauty of the Yorkshire moors. It was brilliant and I loved every second of it. Don't get me wrong, it was not easy. If you made a mistake changing gear then the double de-clutching angel of vengeance would snap the clutch pedal back and whack you very hard in the shin. It really hurt, so you learned to treat the bus with respect. The best bit was a four-hour spin in the morning followed by a magnificent Cornish pasty from a roadside lay-by just outside Hebden Bridge.

My career as a bus driver was actually quite short lived, I did a few shifts, earlies, middles and lates, so I could hold my head up in the canteen when challenged by the lads as to what the hell do you know about it.

I was also known on occasions to jump in and cover the mileage to keep the wheels turning when there were staff shortages. The shifts I did not enjoy were the school runs, – the behaviour of some of the kids beggared belief. You would think that they had been incarcerated in some high security prison, before being allowed out to re-enact a scene from Saint Trinians.

When I hit 50 I was expected to renew my license, but by then I had left the day-to-day world of bus operations and joined the new world of uTrack where driving a bus was no longer required. However, I never lost my enjoyment of jumping on a bus and going for a ride around, watching the world go by and just enjoying the experience for what it was. I actually think that there are a fair few people, especially elderly people, who have a free bus pass and use the bus as a means of social interaction. Sadly in today's world

Image: Christian Mackie Unsplash

a lot of people are so isolated, where they can be surrounded by people but have no human interaction. The bus allows people that interaction, to communicate which is the most basic of human needs. So, I make no apologies for admitting that I like, on occasions, nothing better than catching the bus.

One of the best and most interesting routes is the famous number 11, the Outer Circle as it is known, that circumnavigates the city of Birmingham. It takes in all districts – rich and poor. On this journey you can digest the rich diversity and multi-culturism of this great city, good, bad and occasionally ugly. But, it is real life, warts and all.

People watching is always interesting, we cannot help ourselves. The good old bus gives everyone the chance to get out and about and see the world in all its glory.

So, if you find yourself at a loose end why not do yourself a favour and catch a bus.

The Darkness of Depot Humour!

Well it is that time of year again, the UK's premier bus and coach event. I have lost track of the number of events that I have attended. I vaguely recall, back in the '80s, taking one of my Hereford drivers to the show as he won the ROSCO Safe Driving Award, which was quite some achievement. His name was Les, he was a very quiet man who sadly suffered from skin cancer. This had resulted in some rather nasty blemishes to his head and as a result he

always used to wear a cloth cap. As a result, his nickname was Andy Capp. For some years I didn't realise his nickname was Andy Capp after the famous newspaper cartoon.

No, in my innocence and naivety I just assumed that it was the typical dark humour of the canteen and due to my newness to the local Hereford accent I thought they called him 'Handicap' due to his medical condition. In a similar vein, any unfortunate medical conditions were also seized upon, and of course the more intimate and embarrassing the better. Hence, the poor chap, who as I recall did not stay for long, who was simply called 'One'.

Now, you may be forgiven for thinking in 2014 that this may be a reference to the BBC One show that went out weekdays. But no, this was the 80s and the 'One' reference was indeed related to his full nickname, which was actually 'One-bollock Boyd'. Folklore has it that apparently at one point there were two drivers in the depot called Boyd, so a system needed to be found to give them individual nicknames. Looking back it is wrong on so many levels. Firstly, he took serious umbrage at being addressed as 'One-bollock Boyd'. So, it was agreed amongst the lads that they would shorten it to 'One'. Hardly a charitable act, as all it ever did was remind the poor man of his terrible misfortune on a daily basis.

After he had left to relocate to South Wales I found out that to make matters worse, he actually had never lost such a member in the first place and he was in fact the proud owner of two said appendages. Indeed, the rumours started when he went to hospital to have a minor operation on an ingrowing toe nail.

Depot humour being what it was 'One-toenail Boyd' was never going to cut the mustard and the unfortunate title stuck.

As for me, I was given a number of nicknames, some kind some not, but the one that I liked the most was 'Sergeant Wilson', due to my habit of asking drivers if they would mind awfully doing some overtime as we were in danger of losing mileage.

Looking back, it could have been an awful lot worse!

The Joy of a Hat
First Impressions

The start of my career in the Bus Industry was in 1983. I recall reporting for duty at the rather grand Head Office of the West Yorkshire Road Car Company. The training office was located adjacent to the Stray, the name given to the lovely park that lies in the centre of the very nice town of Harrogate, nestling in 'God's own county' – Yorkshire.

On my first day, I was instructed to report to the Company Training Officer, the lovely and glamorous Mrs Kate Liversedge.

I was dressed in my number one suit and was also sporting a rather smart, grey Crombie coat and trilby hat. My mum and dad had taken me to Moss Bros gentleman's outfitters in Birmingham. My dad had advised me that a hat was an essential piece of equipment, suggesting managerial qualities apparently. It

also allowed me to be able to doff my hat at any ladies that I might encounter.

Looking back it was a nice, sentimental touch that I thought would be valuable, it also had the added benefit of keeping my head warm, whilst I resided 'Up North'. So, suited and booted, there I was primed and ready to start my new career as a Senior Management Trainee of the then mighty National Bus Company. As I climbed the old wooden stairs to the Training Officer's office, I knocked on the door at 08:59 exactly. Punctuality, as you would expect, was vital.

As I entered the office I was greeted by an extremely attractive young lady who was called Linda, she was Mrs Liversedge's secretary. Somewhat taken aback at the vision of beauty sat before me, I formally introduced myself, and of course did the decent thing and doffed my hat. This was greeted with a charming smile and a suggestion of a small snigger, before she asked me to take a seat. She then knocked on the door of the office next door, and duly summoned she entered. To be honest I tried hard not to hear the chat going on, but it was laced with laughing and mirth. And a couple of minutes later, Kate appeared with Linda, I of course jumped up, popped said trilby hat back on my 'napper', as they call it in Geordieland and proceeded to doff said chapeau in the general direction of my new boss.

Yet again a beaming smile and a hint of 'ah how charming that is', fleetingly swept across her face. She was in fairness a really nice and considerate lady, who helped me greatly with my training. She invited me into her office where we went through the company induction. Once complete she then

took me on a tour of the Head Office, where I met the General Manager, Mr Brian Horner, a lovely chap, and everyone else, in every department. This of course led to a significant amount of hat doffing to every lady from the different departments in traffic, engineering, and accounts. The accounts department was populated by a small army of ladies. For reasons best known to myself I attempted an individual doff to each lady. Looking back, one large doff to the assembled masses would probably have been enough, but no, in true trooper fashion, that hat was up and down like a yo-yo on red bull. Funny thing was that each doff solicited the same reaction, a smile followed by a badly hidden snigger.

Looking back, my gestures were a throwback to a lost generation. People did not doff hats anymore, they did back then in the '40s, and early '50s, but not the '80s. I found out some time later, that my hat antics had certainly created an interesting first impression, with an equal measure of charm, and eccentricity apparently.

Interestingly, my dad was a big fan of hats; he had an impressive collection that he used often. His favourite was what I called a

Sooty Gets a Bus Pass

Russian Cossack big grey number, he looked like one of those former Russian Presidents who you used to see standing on the podium at the Russian May Day military celebrations.

The thing was he could get away with it, as the hat accessory was part of his generation. He did it justice in fairness and he had one for every occasion, including the classic Sherlock Holmes deerstalker, which he used to wear when we went to the pub. On his head it commanded respect. Had I sported one, it would have generated derision and sarcasm.

So, my advice to any newcomers about to start their career, do yourself a favour and get yourself a nice hat, to match your smart whistle and flute. And behold the mysterious qualities of courage, chivalry, good manners, and politeness that are the hallmarks of a gentleman, be brave and be slightly deaf, that way you won't hear the aftershocks of giggling that drift behind you.

Oh Dear Lord, just when exactly do the sands of time creep up and suddenly bite you in the bottom?

To elaborate, I was minding my own business, as you do, just aimlessly wandering through the wallpaper that is Facebook when I came across a post from my good friend, 'Mines a bacon butty', none other than the one and only Mr. Phil Tonks. The title gave away the plot immediately.

Sooty gets a Bus Pass.

I couldn't believe it; one of my childhood icons, Sooty, having reached the grand old age of 65 received his free bus pass, which he used to attend an interview on BBC Breakfast.

I mean could he really be 65?

Well yes, he could, and in fairness it's quite sobering when you realise that he was also then entitled to a state pension as well. Sooty for me invokes childish giggling as Sooty, Sweep and Soo indulged in a process of basically arguing with each other until mayhem broke out.

Usually this took the form of Mr Harry Corbett, Sooty's constant companion getting soaked in a combination of both water and cream while the hysterical squeaks from Sooty and his mate Sweep increased to a crescendo. The pair having spent the entire show arguing and winding each other up would then unite and turn on poor old Mr. Corbett.

You always knew what the outcome was

always going to be; it was inevitable, it was just a matter of time. The only voice of reason and I think my first introduction to diplomacy, or emotional intelligence came in the form of the ever-patient Soo.

A voice of reason in a weekly melee of confrontation and whispering where Sooty would have heated discussions with Mr. Corbett before the generally aggressive and mischievous Sweep would release the dogs of war, and out would come the artillery invariably being focused on the hapless Mr Corbett.

When I was a NBC trainee one of my peers and friends was a nice man called Andy, he was from Salford and his dad knew Mr Corbett and they used to occasionally have a beer together. What always made me laugh was that allegedly when Mr. Corbett was off duty and was, as one might expect, asked to do something Sooty like, his standard reply was.

'Sooty is not here right now but if he was he would tell you to bugger off!'

I always thought that the little anecdote was really funny. Gave both Mr Corbett and Sooty a very human quality, as does the concept of iconic legends like Sooty not only receiving but using his free bus pass.

We owe a debt of thanks to both Mr Corbett and his son Matthew who carried on the show long after his dad retired. They made millions laugh and did no one any harm and they built a bit of a legend, and so as we depart I repeat the immortal line...

'Oh no, it's in my eye...

Bye Bye, everyone.'

Homage to the Teddy Boy Coach Driver

Gone But Not Forgotton!

I was once surprised to discover that National Express Coach Company had hit the grand old age of 45 years, not out. I do not really know why, but I always thought of NXC as a young company, maybe because I have grown up with them, since my adolescent years when I used to catch the coach from Digbeth, back in the old days of the original coach station. My formative journeys were usually punctuated by equal measures of uncertainty and fear, uncertainty as to had I actually caught the right coach? Would I actually end up at the destination I intended, or God knows where? Fear due to the generally aggressive and very grumpy, middle-aged men who were the classic coach drivers.

Back then coach driving attracted a certain type of applicant, being very stereotypical and maybe very unfair, my teenage memories recalled rather big, chunky men with a fair bit of gold bling, tattoos and, in some cases, a quiff in homage to the King himself (just in case you have no idea who I am talking about, I refer to Elvis Aaron Presley, aka The King). The quiff may also need some explanation, back in the day this hairstyle was known as a DA, or Duck's Arse., it had its roots back in the heady days of the Teddy Boy. Back in the fifties, long before the advent of the Mods and Rockers, youth culture and teenage gangs consisted of the rock and roll loving, switch blade carrying, young men, who interestingly chose to wear brightly coloured, long coats fashionable during the reign of King Edward - hence, Teddy Boys.

To be fair the men who actually drove the mighty coaches up and down the Nation's highways would have been the right demographic age wise, to have been original Teddy Boys. No surprise really that they carried their heritage with them. I have to say that 45 years on, this breed of driver has, like the Dodo, become extinct, as age and retirement catch up. Who knows, in my more fanciful moments I would like to think that nestling somewhere, probably close to the seaside, is a retirement home for such a rare breed. The Blue Suede Shoes Retirement Home (no hipsters, millenials, or technology welcome, thank you), would cater for the whims and desires of the dooh wop loving, jiving, gents and their good lady wives, suitably equipped in their swirling skirts and tight head bands to dance the night away, jitterbugging their way to a time when they could rock around the clock, until it was time to meet the King himself, waiting patiently at the pearly gates of Graceland itself.

Thinking of these men, I recall one particular chap at my very first ever depot management job, at the tiny depot of Malton, in God's own County of Yorkshire. The main man was a lovely chap who was an Elvis doppelgänger, he was a kindly man who knew what he was doing, and he made my life easy. Although a born and bred Yorkshiremen, such was his adoration for the King, that he used to talk like him. In fact when I first actually met him and was formally introduced he mumbled at me.

"Uh huh, real pleasure to meet you Sir, uh huh".

At first I thought that he had some sort of speech impediment. But, to be fair, I soon realised that this was him, a man comfortable in himself, the King of Malton Depot, and let's be fair I was nothing but a visiting hound dog. I learned a lot from Elvis, he was a man of few words, often a modest uh huh, was as good as it got, but he knew his job and he knew his men and customers.

Looking back I have, after everything, a sneaking fondness and respect for these men. They were from an era, children and teenagers during the war, brought up on rationing, evacuation, air raids, powdered egg, and no bananas. And after the tough, dark days of World War II, and all that went with it, maybe the completely alien world of rock and roll and its individual culture of colour, fashion and self-identity was the exact tonic they needed, who knows. Suffice to say we shall not see their like again, but they did their bit and they carried the baton.

Fair play to that uh huh, thank you very much and uh huh, Elvis has truly left the building.

Nostalgia is Not What it Used to be…

The closure of Hereford Depot got me thinking back at my life and times and I am blessed to enjoy very positive memories and reflections. Yes, of course, I have had my fair share of trials and tribulations. As my dear old dad used to say, 'Into every life a little rain must fall'. Indeed, on occasions I have endured and overcome one or two monsoons, but overall the good Lord has been good to me.

Funnily enough, I found an old magazine called Bus and Coach Management dated June/July 1988, which cost £2.00 back in the day. It contained an article about me, then aged 27, and the recent launch of my brand-new, sparkling fleet of Hereford Hoppers. It was written by a nice gentlemen called Geoffrey Hancock.

It was a great, very upbeat article and the enthusiasm of youth sparkled from the page. I was truly bubbling back in the day, we were on a real roll. Ten of us managers, under

Image: uTrack

the noble leadership of Big Ken Mills, had recently bought out the company and we had a genuine sense that anything was possible, and indeed it was. We were about to make the staff who took the free shares very rich. The £500 holiday pay they used to buy the shares would convert to £35,000 each as the 5p share rocketed to £3.50. That was a whopping 70-fold increase on a free investment when, later that year, we sold the business to Badgerline, who in turn went on to merge with Grampian Regional Transport, who went on to become Firstgroup PLC. The world's largest transport company went on to turn over £7 billion and employ 123,000 people.

Ironically, as I later sat in the main board room at First's London HQ and talked about how uTrack had helped to transform both the Aircoach and Greyhound Companies in Ireland and the entire continent of North America, I realised that my own world had gone full circle.

When I finally left Hereford and went to my next job as District Manager Kidderminster and the Wyre Forest, I was given a very special present. It was a poem written by a man who I had a great deal of time for. His name was Inspector Dave Inman, and he was a third-generation soldier of the Mercian regiment, who joined the Bus Industry when he left the army.

He joined as a driver and then was made an inspector. He was a good man and always, as you would expect, immaculately well turned out. So, on my very last day in charge we all went next door to the Military Club, where the lads and lasses had laid on 'a bit of a do' as they used to say in Hereford.

Dave read the poem to much acclaim as it really did sum me up, i.e. code for *drinks too much beer and can't get up in the morning...* spot on to be fair, but it summed up my relationship with them, and them with me,

Here goes:

There came to Hereford, this northern chap,
From the distant Ribble vale,
And from the start his greatest attribute,
Was drinking local ale.

He came to manage country men,
With his smile and curly hair,
You could always trespass within his den,
In the knowledge he would be fair.

With winning ways and listening ear,
He dispelled all the sneering smirks,
That he could put Hereford on the map,
For he was from a long line of Birks.

And so my friends it came to pass,
That he took the bull by the horns,
He took the garage from strength to strength,
But not by getting up at dawn.

The debt that we all now owe this lad,
With the secure years of the past,
There are those amongst us who must be sad,
That he is moving on at last.
But all has not been forgotten,

From the drivers to a clerk,
We have all been happy,
To be managed by a Birk...

Priceless, you really cannot make it up. Thanks a lot Hereford, and Dave.

I Would Like To Thank...
My Parents, My Agent

So, it came to pass that the red carpet was rolled out, the paparazzi were lined up and the celebs congregated, and then I woke up. Yes playmates, after some 18 months of planning and detailed preparation, the CILT film premiere was finally shown to a selected audience at the world-famous Millbrook proving ground in Buckinghamshire.

The film was designed to deliver a powerful safety message to senior leaders of the business communities within CILT and, although initially focused on the road freight and passenger sectors, it was equally applicable to any board and any industry. It all came down to what was important; the commercial interests of the business or the recognition of putting safety at the heart of the business. It also analysed the moral, economic and legal (MEL) aspects of the debate.

The day at Millbrook had a great array of professional speakers who gave clarity and light to these fundamental questions. From my personal point of view, I had seen the film so many times that I had really lost touch with how those seeing it for the first time might actually perceive it.

So, it was particularly interesting and indeed sobering to hear Mrs Beverley Bell describe it as harrowing, especially the scene where a cyclist gets killed. As she said, 'you just know what is going to happen next' and 'It made the hair on the back of my neck stand up', I knew what she meant, as there was an almost tragic inevitability followed by a very graphic scene after the accident happens.

The purpose of the day was, quite simply, to raise awareness of the potential dangers posed on a daily basis to vulnerable road

users and how the leadership communities can implement policies that will make the streets of this land safer for all of us. What was also interesting was to note that it is not just the obvious vulnerable road users who are prone to danger.

Any one of us who put headphones on and then proceed to cross roads, ride bicycles or drive cars while sending text messages, or indeed allow ourselves to get distracted in any way, shape or form, are actually putting ourselves and others at risk every time we succumb to temptation.

I did a little experiment as I was stuck on the M1 going home after the event. I watched how many motorists, stuck not moving, were either reading messages or sending texts, and it was quite staggering. I would say half were engaged in some sort of distraction. Don't get me wrong, I am guilty as charged, of course I am, but from then on I made a determined effort to be stronger.

Breaking And Entering...
Stop Coach Thief!

On one of those warm nights when I couldn't sleep, I had a late night foray into Facebook. I'd woken up and decided that I needed to do something to get me back to sleep. I thought the easiest option for a half asleep brain was to slip into the brain fog that is Faceache, as my friend likes to call it.

As I trundled my way through the nonsense that flicked past me, suddenly I stumbled across a photo of my dear old bus depot in Friar Street, Hereford. The photo showed the bulldozer just at the point where it finally levelled the old drivers' canteen. The faded green paint, which incidentally was faded when I first got there back in 1986, was all that could be identified in the mangled wreckage that for 95 years served generations of the good folk of the lovely city of Hereford. A city of great heritage, indeed I was fortunate enough to be invited to the 650th Mayor-making ceremony that took place in 1995.

Reflecting, as you do on those happy events, it also got me thinking about some of the less pleasant and happy memories from when I was the Depot Manager at Hereford back in the days when it was part of Midland Red West. One vague memory that came bouncing back at me was when I received a phone call at 05:00 from my right hand man, Howard Pritchard.

Howard was the first man into the depot

every day. He opened the door and started the daily ritual of getting buses, drivers, mechanics, and cleaners lined up to get the services out on time. Howard met and greeted all and sundry. He was completely reliable, a decent and kind man. He'd never married, had no family other than his sister, took no holidays and, for me, he was a priceless asset and a good friend.

Anyway, as ever I digress. As soon as the phone rang at 05:00 I knew that this was not good news.

"Gaffer, you better get your backside here, there has been a break-in, it's chaos, the Rozzers are on the way."

Bleary eyed, I made my way down to the depot, and Howard was not exaggerating. Persons unknown had taken an acetylene torch to the safe and removed the door. Quite an achievement given the thickness of the beast. Furthermore, there was water everywhere as they had been cooling the area down.

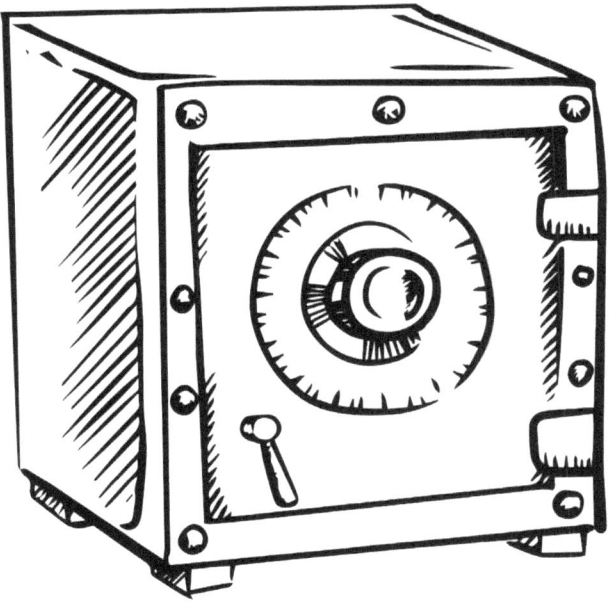

It was clear they knew exactly what they were doing. So, the Police turned up and sealed it all off while we made the best of getting on with the day job.

That reminded me of another occasion when we had unwanted intruders. This time though it was in the form of a coach thief; the short version goes as follows. One Friday afternoon we received a fax advising all bus companies in the South of England that a National Express Coach had been stolen from Battersea Coach Station, in London. At about 17:00 Gerry Phillips, my best mate and senior mechanic, ran into my office as I was putting my coat on.

"That stolen coach is here. The bloke is refuelling it." He exclaimed.

I looked up and sure enough at the top end was a white NX Coach with the driver.

I immediately ran towards it and the driver drove the coach at speed towards the exit. It became apparent that he was not going to stop, so I had to literally dive out of his way, and was covered in wet, slimy diesel gunk. The next thing was I heard a large bang. This was matey boy slamming on the brakes as the two fitters, Gerry and Tony Andrews, managed to shut the exit doors. As you can understand I was not happy, so I jumped up and legged it after the driver who had run into the narrow gap left when the doors shut.

The next bit is still hazy, but all I recall is me chasing and catching this guy who had legged it across the road into the churchyard of Saint Nicholas Church. The churchyard had a large steel fence, behind which was the outer ring road of the city. It was 17:00 and the traffic was gridlocked. One minute I am standing right in front of this guy and the next he is lying on the floor. Witnesses stated that when I confronted this chap, he attempted to hit me with a suitcase he was holding, I then blocked the strike with my left hand (uchi uke jodan, middle level block in Shotokan Karate). I then kicked him in the stomach (mae geri chudan), and as he was going down I punched him in the head (kizami zuki jodan). He then lay motionless on the floor as I looked up to see a sea of static car drivers and passengers watching a quick re-enactment of Enter The Dragon.

The two lads, Gerry and Tony, observed the whole thing, so the three of us picked him up and frogmarched him back to the depot where the police were called. Statements were taken, he was arrested, and I ended up with a commendation for bravery from the Police, along with Gerry and Tony.

Make a Note of That Man's Name Sergeant Major

I was thinking recently of some of the many varied and wonderful things that I have been involved with in my life-long career in the Bus Industry. One of the strange consequences of being born into the Bus Industry as I was, is that I have never really known anything else. This, of course, makes me utterly biased as I have nothing to cross-reference life with.

However, one thing is very clear, the world has changed dramatically over the course of my lifetime. When I was born in 1960, my dad was an area manager at Southdown Motor Services in Brighton. Back in the day, bus travel was at its premium with special excursions being operated to manage the thousands of people who popped over for the day and wanted to see the delights of the Pier, Beachy Head and the Lanes, etc.

In truth, it was an age of different values. The Second World War had only been over for 15 years and, at last, Britain was on the up. As Harold Macmillan famously said, we had never had it so good. Life at the time had a much gentler pace and I recall that, at Christmas, huge depot parties would be organised, with my parents as the main guests, and the four children would be turned out in our Sunday best with strict instructions as to how to behave.

In some senses these were Victorian values where children were seen and not heard, but that was just as their generation had been educated. I am not sure what my dad would have made of today's Twitter, Facebook and text world with its need for instant gratification. Perplexed and bemused I suspect.

The Bus Industry has always had strong connections with the military and the structure historically was similar, with inspectors being replaced by former NCOs. I came across many ex-servicemen who found a natural empathy with the predictable structure that a bus man's life had to offer. Many of them were automatic selections as supervisors and inspectors and, of course, the main man was always the chief inspector.

One man stands out in my child-like eyes as they were at the time. I was at primary school in Harborne in Birmingham and one day a car pulled up to our house to pick my father up, who had recently been appointed as the Traffic Manager for the mighty Midland Red Bus Company. As I opened the door, the sunlight was obliterated as a monster dressed in black seemed to occupy the whole earth.

I looked up to see this giant boom at me, "Hello son, is your dad at home?"

Well, of course, I did the only thing that you could and legged it, just as my dad appeared and stopped me.

"Austin, what are you doing? Say hello to Chief Inspector Hanlon."

At this, the man-mountain removed his gleaming black hat with its shiny silver badge and tucked it under his other arm, as you would having been the former Regimental Sergeant Major of the Grenadier Guards.

"Hello," he boomed and offered the huge hand of friendship,

"Good morning, Sir," I replied somewhat sheepishly, at which point he smiled, turned on his heels and marched out with my dad.

He was a bit of a legend within the old Midland Red Bus Company and his job was to instil order with the junior ranks, as he called them. His physicality and bearing were immense - one of those rare characters that you instinctively want on your side in times of trouble. He carried the bearing of a man who could dish out equal measures of support and threat, depending on what you were doing and how you were behaving.

In stark contrast was a chap who once worked for me, he was also an ex-army man, but he was well-known for his pugilistic skills rather than diplomacy. One of the things that I do recall about him was that he had the word 'love' tattooed on the fingers of his left hand. On his right hand, he had once had the word 'hate'. The trouble was that, sadly, the little finger on his right hand had been amputated after an accident, leaving the immortal legend 'Love and Hat'.

That doesn't really have the same effect, does it?

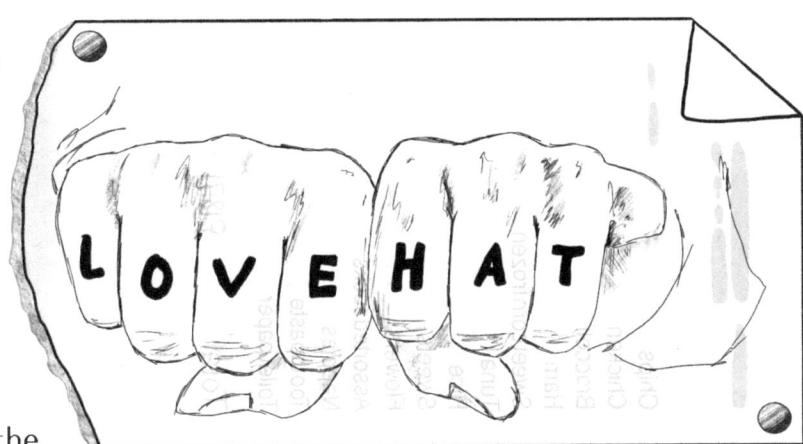

Farewell My Dear Friends...
My Last Solo Utrack Blog

All good things, as they say, come to an end, and so it is in my life and times.

Sadly, after a combination of the accelerated chemotherapy treatments, together with the evolution and development of uTrack mean that it was time for me to lay down the pen and say adios to the uTrack blog.

I have to say that it was an honour and a privilege to have been allowed to write about anything and everything over the years since the very first blog on the January 30th, 2012, a fair few years ago now. I am pleased that over the years and I maintained my personal goal of three blogs a week. And I will be eternally grateful that Eamonn and Conor allowed me to indulge myself with writing and venting about anything and everything. It has truly been a deep, rich, and wonderful experience that I will be forever grateful for experiencing.

Over the years I have laughed more than I could ever have imagined as I remembered experiences, people, situations, and life that you could not honestly make up. Yes it has also been a vehicle for change and reform for which I make no apologies.

I am an absolutely committed advocate and champion for both the Bus and Coach Industry and the Chartered Institute of Logistics and Transport. I am devoted to championing their cause and future. I was, after all, born quite literally into both institutions, due to the influence of my mentor and hero, my dad, John Austin Birks. It is also strangely fitting that I ended this journey on the anniversary of his parting, for me a nice rounding of the circle.

However, these blogs I hope will live on within this book. I fervently hope that this book is not simply a social documentary of my life and times over these turbulent years, but also a source of laughter. Also, if I dare say it, may it be a chronicle of lessons that I learned in the wonderful Bus and Coach Industry, and a guide for those who might wish to join in the future. It is as my dear old dad always said an industry about people, and he was so right.

I offer my thanks, my dear reader chums, for your kindness in taking the time to read my nonsense, it has been wonderful, and I genuinely and sincerely thank you all.

Farewell and goodbye.

www.ingramcontent.com/pod-product-compliance
Lightning Source LLC
Chambersburg PA
CBHW041504220426

43661CB00016B/1250